Seniors to Juniors

A Collection of Waterloo Hockey Stories

Tim Harwood

First Collected Together 2025
BTSCP Books – Waterloo, IA

ISBN: 979-8218769345

For the 2024/25 Black Hawks,
champions in every way that matters.

Other Books About Waterloo Sports

Black Hawks Chronicle; Five Decades of Teams, Games, and Players

The Legion Team; Forgotten Hockey in Waterloo, 1927-1930

Ball Hawks; The Arrival and Departure of the NBA in Iowa

50 Thanksgivings; Waterloo's Hockey Holiday

CONTENTS

Author's Note

The articles in this book are collected from 20 years of covering Black Hawks hockey. All of them have appeared before. Each story is included as it was originally produced, except minor changes for stylistic consistency. A note at the beginning of each feature provides details regarding the original publication and – where useful – context which helps to explain more about the time when it was written or related events which have followed since. As of 2025, some articles are still easily accessible from their original sources, but others are not. It's hard to predict if or when online content might disappear (even though conventional wisdom suggests that once something is on the internet, it never goes away), so thank you for enjoying these stories – and in the process, preserving them – even if you have seen some of the content before. Thanks also to the Waterloo Black Hawks for encouraging the publication of this book, and to all the players, coaches, and others who shared their perspectives on hockey in the Cedar Valley.

Seniors To Juniors

The Evolving USHL

Originally published in The Iowa Sports Connection *Volume 11, Issue 8 – November 2009. The USHL Fall Classic did not become a regular season event until the autumn of 2018.*

All 14 United States Hockey League teams made their way to Sioux City during the final weekend of September. The annual USHL Fall Classic offered a three-day preseason field laboratory for coaches to run their final roster experiments. With all of the clubs in one place, Tyson Events Center was a magnet for NHL and college scouts looking for their next big star among the 16-20-year-olds on the ice. It also attracted Jim Coyle and Tim Taylor, who played in a very different United States Hockey League more than 40 years ago.

Both were members of the Waterloo Black Hawks in the 1960s. Coyle came to Waterloo in the organization's inaugural season, 1962/63, after graduating from the University of Michigan. Taylor was cut from the 1964 U.S. Olympic team following his college career at Harvard. He first appeared on the Black Hawks' roster in November of 1963. Many players in the USHL at that time were coming from college or amateur ranks to the semi-professional "senior league."

"You want to remember back in those days, there were only six NHL teams," says Coyle, "So if you didn't make the big time, you could either become a hockey bum and move from team to team and eke out a meager living, or you could take an opportunity like the Waterloo Black Hawks, where they found you a job, and you could build a career from that."

Those career opportunities led many USHL players of the era to settle into their new communities. Road trips were organized so teams could still make it to their nine-to-five jobs on Monday. Don't confuse the old USHL with a beer league, however. Taylor says he and his teammates continued play a high level of hockey.

"Everybody worked and lived in the community," Taylor says "and we were able, with our setup, to practice every day. Those were great years in my life. I was still aspiring to play a better brand of hockey. I learned a lot from a lot of the veteran players who I had a chance to play with."

On non-game days, Taylor worked for the Waterloo Recreation Commission and helped create the youth hockey program that still exists in the community. Coyle was a credit manager with Iowa Public Service (MidAmerican Energy). Other Black Hawks were school teachers, insurance salesmen, plumbers, industrial workers, or involved in a variety of other trades and professions.

"I'll never forget [Head Coach] Oakie Brumm telling the Board that they'll know they're successful when somebody quits hockey because of their job," recalls Coyle. "That was their philosophy, for us to become part of the community, and I think they were extremely successful."

Not every Black Hawk settled permanently in Waterloo. Taylor eventually returned east, and after working as an assistant hockey coach at his alma matter, he spent nearly three decades as the head coach for rival Yale. In that time, he also coached U.S. Olympic hockey teams, as an assistant in 1984 and in the lead role in 1994. Taylor still works in the game as an executive with USA Hockey, helping to guide the U.S. National Team Development Program, whose Under-17 and Under-18 teams will be part of the USHL this season.

Coyle and many others did remain in Waterloo, however. The net-minder left the crease for the last time in 1973/74, but continued to work within the utility industry. In the mid-1980s, he was transferred to Sioux City. When he retired, Coyle was Vice President of Customer Service for MidAmerican and now sees some of his retired teammates living in Florida. His departure from the Black Hawks came at the eve of the USHL's transition to junior hockey.

With NHL expansion and the creation of the rival World Hockey Association, many players who might have continued their careers at the senior level had a chance to make it in the pros. In search of a new talent source, team organizers merged their clubs with the Midwest Junior Hockey League. By 1979/80, there were no more senior players on the loop. The transition wasn't always easy for fans used to a more polished level of play, but as the game grew in the United States, the USHL evolved into the nation's top junior circuit.

"It was certainly a different level of hockey, but no more or less entertaining," reflects Taylor.

Watching players who will almost all climb from the USHL to the NCAA, Coyle seems to agree.

"When you look at the value of a scholarship today, these young kids out here are hustling for some big bucks and great opportunities. A college education today is awful expensive. There's a lot of pressure on those young men."

One thing hasn't changed among USHL players. They still leave home and come to Waterloo and other towns in the league from across the nation, drawn by the opportunity to keep playing the game they love.

Once Teammates, Now Fans

Pavelski's Pals from Waterloo Pull for Him, Dallas

This feature first appeared on waterlooblackhawks.com September 21, 2020, as the Dallas Stars met the Tampa Bay Lightning in the Stanley Cup Final. The article was republished in the Waterloo Courier *the following day under the title* 'Big' Pavelski Fans.

Over the last 14 seasons, hockey fans have learned a lot about Joe Pavelski. During that time, he has played in over 1,200 NHL regular season, Stanley Cup playoff, or Winter Olympic games. Pavelski has been a team captain. He has skated in All-Star events. Tonight, he'll be on the ice for Game Two in the 2020 Stanley Cup Final; it's the second time he has helped a team into the shadow of the most coveted trophy in sports.

Matt Fornataro didn't have the benefit of reviewing Pavelski's expansive resume when he formed a first impression of his future teammate back in the summer of 2002.

"When I first saw Joe in a scrimmage game for training camp in Waterloo, I said to myself 'That's him…?'" Fornataro recently remembered.

They spent two years together with the Black Hawks, winning a United States Hockey League division title that spring before going on to celebrate a Clark Cup championship in 2004. Fornataro had discarded his initial assessment of Pavelski long before those achievements. In fact, Fornataro remembers already being impressed as their first season together was beginning.

"Being around him every day, you started to realize that he was a special player. The biggest things were his attention to detail and his hunger to grow and learn. He was always staying late and doing more than the rest of us, but it was never about him. Joe understood at a young age that if he made himself better, he could help the team more. TEAM is always more important than individual, and Joe has always understood that."

Defenseman Reid Cashman was on hand too, as the 2002/03 Black Hawks were forming. The arc of Cashman's career – like Pavelski's – also included rising to the NHL; the former assistant coach of the Washington

Capitals is preparing for his first season as head coach of Dartmouth's men's hockey program. While making arrangements for the college campaign, Cashman was also willing to reminisce.

"Our year together – from Coach O'Handley's first meeting – Coach hammered home two points that were going to become part of the identity of the Waterloo Black Hawks' organization. 1) Compete every day and compete in every aspect of your life, on the ice and off. Always strive to get better; always strive to win. 2) If the team has success, then individuals will have success.

"I think Joe has won as much as he has, and been as successful as he has, in large part due to him living these two ideas."

Cashman and Pavelski were among the most successful Black Hawks as the 2002/03 season ended. The defenseman from Red Wing, Minnesota, notched 47 points in 56 games and tied for the league scoring lead among players at his position. Cashman claimed a spot on the All-USHL Second Team before going on to an All-American college career at Quinnipiac and time spent playing as a pro in North America and Europe.

Pavelski was the 2003 USHL Rookie of the Year and took a step toward the NHL that summer when the San Jose Sharks drafted him 205th overall. After Pavelski had scored 36 goals and earned more than a point per game (69 in 60 appearances), hindsight indicates that it was a remarkable value pick.

Forward Garrett Regan played with the Hawks before and after the Minnesota high school hockey season in 2002/03 and came to Waterloo fulltime in 2003/04, joining a club which had begun establishing a new culture of winning.

"Joe is just a winner," says Regan. "He doesn't make a big deal about it, that's just all he knows and all he expects. It's fun to be around those types of players and people, because there isn't any other option for them."

Regan says Pavelski's impact came with the way he played the game rather than what he said. Serving as Waterloo's captain in 2003/04, Pavelski was the steadying influence as the Hawks struggled through the early months of the season. For a time, the talented team was at the bottom of the standings before rallying in the second half of the schedule to reach the playoffs, then defeating both division champions on the way to the Clark Cup.

Regan was the Hawks' third-highest scorer during the playoff run with 11 points. He and Pavelski each scored six times.

Zach Bearson was one of the youngest players on the 2003/04 team. He would later become a Black Hawks captain, an NHL Draft pick, and a Wisconsin Badger, following Pavelski's trail in each of those distinctions.

While Pavelski's teammates consistently reinforce the idea that his leadership was primarily by example, some of Pavelski's words have also stuck with Bearson.

"He told me, sitting on his balcony in Madison, that he thought about hockey like he thought about golf (which he is clearly awesome at also!)…that to be truly great, you have to be well-rounded, capable of hitting all the shots.

"I think his career probably reflects that mature approach. I think about that metaphor all the time in the professional/business world: just improving in all facets, never being satisfied. Give credit to 21-year-old Joe with that sage wisdom and advice."

Pete MacArthur tied Pavelski as the 2003/04 Hawks' playoff scoring leader with a dozen points. The forward – one of a limited number of Pavelski's Waterloo's teammates who is still playing (MacArthur signed a contract with Orlando of the ECHL in July) – offered his assessment of Pavelski's talents, which have improved with time.

"Truthfully, I think he has just fine-tuned his skill set over the years. He was never an unreal skater, blowing by people or dangling guys. His Hockey I.Q. is off the charts, which allows him to constantly be in the perfect, or close-to perfect, position."

Fornataro says Pavelski's game has evolved, providing new opportunities to contribute, first as a veteran for the Sharks, and this season with the Dallas Stars.

"If you look early in his career, his goals were a lot more off the rush or one-timers from the dot; he scored more goals with his shot. As the game has changed, he has found ways to continue to produce by finding new ways to score goals. This is where tipping pucks comes from. He worked at it for years before it started to benefit his game. A key lesson for any young athlete is that these skills take time to cultivate, practice, and perfect."

That ability to continue developing provided Pavelski with the chance to play in his 1,000th NHL regular season game last fall. He has remained relevant long enough for a teammate like Cashman to make a substantial climb up the coaching ladder and toward a reunion of sorts when the Sharks met Washington prior to this season.

"Seventeen years later [after Waterloo], we were both in the NHL," Cashman notes. "He'd always look up and give a little wink if there was a faceoff by our bench. We would catch up after the game; those were special moments, [although] we got rained out of golf both years when we were on the road in San Jose."

Now after his first season with Dallas, Pavelski has exploded for nine goals and 14 points in the postseason after a modest 14 goals and 31 points during the COVID-19-shortened campaign. Even without the recent tangible scoring production, Pavelski's former Waterloo teammates believe his contribution has had a substantial impact on helping the Stars into the Stanley Cup Final.

"They are lucky to have a guy with a lot of experience, a guy who is certainly motivated, and a guy who has won at every level he's ever played at," says Bearson, who coincidentally stepped out of Pavelski's footsteps and moved to Dallas to take a job there (outside of hockey) before Pavelski arrived last summer. "You know he will show up in the moment when [he is] needed the most."

"Joe is a gamer," adds MacArthur. "That experience he has is invaluable to the Stars. He takes some pressure off Benn/Seguin/Radulov with his style of play and really makes the team that much deeper."

Regan and Fornataro expressed what all of Pavelski's former teammates are feeling as the Stars-Tampa Bay Lightning series continues.

"We look forward to Joe having a great Cup Final and hopefully bringing it home!" Regan says.

"I think Joe has touched so many people in so many ways throughout his career that the culmination of him winning the Cup will mean so much to so many," notes Fornataro. "He has a lot of people pulling for him."

With the Stars leading Tampa Bay after a 4-1 Game One victory Saturday, the shadow of the Cup could become a little thicker tonight. Game Two begins at 7 p.m.

Don't Call Them "Little" Brothers

Another article from The Iowa Sports Connection *Volume 10, Issue 1 – March, 2008.*

Nobody mispronounced Scott Pavelski's name when he arrived in Waterloo late last summer to join the Black Hawks for the preseason. For his part, Pavelski had a good idea what to expect from the United States Hockey League.

Five years earlier, his older brother, Joe, led the Hawks to their then-best regular season record, following that up in 2003/04 by captaining the team to a Clark Cup championship and being named USA Hockey's Junior Player of the Year. In the spring of 2006, the elder Pavelski assisted on both goals during the Wisconsin Badgers' 2-1 win against Boston College in the NCAA's national championship game. He was playing in the NHL for the San Jose Sharks before Thanksgiving that fall.

That's a lot to live up to.

"People watch you a little bit more closely," Scott Pavelski says, "So you know that they're going to criticize you a little bit more if you're not doing what they thought you could."

Still, the 18-year-old forward from Central Wisconsin feels like he was more prepared for the rigors of the country's top junior hockey league after seeing his brother rise to the challenge. Familiarity with the environment and coaches made the jump to Waterloo natural.

"I always did what [Joe] did, like we both also golf together, and I think a big part of that is I look up to him as a role model. So the reason I'm following the same path is to be like him someday."

Pavelski isn't the only Black Hawk with an accomplished older brother. Defenseman Mike Marcou had the opportunity to skate with brother James Marcou last year in Waterloo as James was having the best offensive season of any Black Hawk in more than a decade. The Marcous had previously played together in the Atlantic Junior Hockey League and are on track to once again wear the same uniform next fall with the UMass Minutemen.

"I think it will be great, playing junior hockey with my brother, and college," Marcou says. "Not many kids get to do that and I think it will just be fun, and a lot easier for me too."

Defenseman Blake Kessel enjoyed growing up in a competitive sports family, including not only his older brother Phil, but also his younger sister, Amanda.

"Everyone's competitive no matter what it is, it's golf, it's tennis, it's hockey, even card games…that's what's been great though, having a close family. Phil, Amanda, and I, we've always been close and that's what's really been kind of special."

Blake says he has learned more about the off-ice side of hockey since Phil was selected in the first round of the NHL Draft by the Boston Bruins in 2006.

"One thing is just taking it more seriously. It's his job now, and it's definitely something, if I want it to be my job in the future, I have to change everything the way that he has," Kessel reflects. "Over the years, we changed our diets around. We changed our workout routine, so it's really kind of a good thing that I can see him go through it and kind of learn from him."

While Phil Kessel appears consistently in SportsCenter highlights after Bruins games, Blake Kessel says it's Amanda who might be the most skilled and the fiercest competitor. This winter, she played for the United States team at the World Women's Under-18 Championship, bringing home a gold medal from the tournament in Alberta. Amanda scored the final goal in Team USA's 5-2 victory over Canada during the finale and finished tied for third in team scoring.

John Lee, also a Black Hawk defenseman, says he has benefited since his brother Brian was taken with the ninth pick of the 2005 Draft by the Ottawa Senators.

"We skate in the summer together, so that really helps a lot," says Lee, adding, "Summer is a big key in working out together and shooting pucks and getting on the ice."

That work has paid off; Lee, like Blake Kessel, was drafted last summer. Asked what he would tell younger siblings who inherit big expectations, Lee says everyone has the choice to go their own way.

"I think it's a little bit harder to do the same thing, just because you do have guys that are going to call you out and say you're there because of your brother or your sister. You just have to enjoy what you're doing, and if you're not having fun, it's not worth doing."

Cates vs. Cates

This feature was the cover story for the February 2018 edition of Hawk Tawk Mag-e-Zine, *the team's season ticket newsletter. Jackson and Noah Cates both went on to play in the NHL for the Philadelphia Flyers.*

The puck slipped to Jackson Cates in the high slot.

Late in the opening period during the first game after Christmas, the Black Hawks were on the power play. Working as the fourth forward on that special teams unit, Cates stepped toward the net, bounced off a defender, and – while losing balance – slid a perfect pass to Garrett Wait, who scored into an open side.

It was a brilliant play at an opportune time. Cates helped Waterloo take a 1-0 lead on a night when his parents, grandpa, and friends were on hand for the game.

His little brother was at the rink in Omaha, too…playing for the Lancers.

"He keeps his cards pretty close to the vest, but the smile tells a lot," said Hawks Coach PK O'Handley, thinking back to watching Waterloo's leading goal scorer during that game.

"Of course, I got the smile [from him that] night, and rightfully so. Jackson had a heck of a game and we needed that too."

Cates also scored in the second period, and the Hawks prevailed 3-0.

Throughout the holidays, there had been some buildup around the Cates household as Jackson and his brother, Noah (16 months younger), prepared to square off for the first time in the United States Hockey League.

"It was more family and friends that talked about it than us talking about it," Jackson remembered. "We didn't really like, brag, or anything, but it was definitely fun knowing that we would play each other next...especially after playing with him my whole life, on the same line and everything."

And the number one question the Cates brothers heard during the season of "peace on earth and goodwill toward men?"

"A lot of people asked if we were going to fight each other and stuff like that," Jackson remembered. "We joked around and said 'Yeah, you never know.' It was fun."

Back in Waterloo after Christmas, Cates heard about the matchup from his coaches and teammates.

"[We] ribbed him a little bit, and he just gave his normal smile," said O'Handley, "so I would guess the older brother wanted to let the little brother know who's in charge."

Whatever Cates had expected, the reality of taking the ice in these circumstances was a little different than what he had experienced during his first season-and-a-half in the league.

"At times it was weird," Jackson conceded. "When he was on the ice and I was on the bench, I would just get caught watching him sometimes. It was different, that's for sure."

Just over a week later, in Omaha again, the elder Cates would make another spectacular play, but it was Noah who celebrated last that night.

The Hawks trailed 2-1 with under a minute remaining and were shorthanded. Noah had assisted on both Omaha goals, and the Lancers were in position to level the series as tension built among the 3,300 fans at Ralston Arena.

Waterloo pulled Matej Tomek to the bench, and with 30 seconds to go, Jackson brought the puck into the Lancer zone. Drawing all the attention from the Omaha defense, he was knocked to a knee as he moved toward the top of the crease. Yet Cates still connected on a feed to Jack Drury, who snapped a shot to the back of the net as defensemen and goaltender Vincent Purpura sprawled in vain to stop the puck.

A jubilant celebration did not last long. Omaha won the game 34 seconds into overtime.

Besides delivering the game-saving goal on Jackson's assist, Drury might have also provided the best remark about the Cates-against-Cates series.

"Drury told me, then my brother told me after the game that Drury had said to him, 'Your mom likes Jackson better.' I thought that was pretty funny."

When they were on the ice directly against each other, Jackson says his interactions with Noah were a little more subtle.

"We ended up playing each other on the ice a good amount in all three games. We faced off against each other a few times and would just say a couple words and take the draw...just like 'What's up?' or something, nothing too much."

The rubber game in the series was played at Young Arena on January 14th. The Cates family was again well-represented in the stands for the Sunday afternoon matchup.

Noah scored the first goal midway through the opening period, but Wait tied the score before intermission, and Bobby Trivigno gave Waterloo the lead during the first minute of the second period. The Hawks would stay in front from that point onward, eventually securing two points by way of the 5-2 final.

"Over the summer, I'll have the bragging rights, so that'll be good," Jackson smiled.

That assumes the Hawks and Lancers don't meet again after the regular season schedule runs out.

"You never know with playoffs, but that could be a little more feisty," Jackson admits. "I feel like it could get a little more personal in the playoffs compared to the first three games, but I guess we'll have to find out."

On a longer timeline, Jackson and Noah will be teammates again when they both wear the maroon and gold of Minnesota-Duluth. That's where another set of brothers with a tie to Waterloo have been reunited this winter. Freshman and sophomore Mikey and Joey Anderson skated against each other in the USHL during January of 2016 when Mikey was a Hawk and Joey was with the National Team Development Program.

"I know they're loving it together up in Duluth," Jackson noted.

And at least for the moment, he will be the undisputed titleholder in the Cates family, although that was a fact he downplayed.

"I just thought it was fun to see all of my family and friends come down to Waterloo when we played each other. We got pictures with everyone, and I got to talk to my brother after the game, so it was pretty cool."

It's definitely easier to be a gracious big brother when the little brother knows who's in charge.

“You Guys the Hansons?”

A Story of Old Time Hockey in Waterloo

This article first appeared on waterlooblackhawks.com on April 11, 2024.

In October of 1973, Dave Swick made a decision that changed the course of hockey history as we know it.

Swick was a longtime Black Hawks forward who had just become Waterloo’s new head coach. That summer, the team had been purchased by local residents through a community stock drive. The first regular season game was a little more than a week away. Then three gangly kids arrived from Minnesota.

A few years later, Jack, Steve, and Jeff Carlson would go on to undying fame as the inspiration for the Hanson Brothers in the 1977 movie *Slap Shot* (with Steve and Jeff actually playing a version of themselves in the film).

For a few days, they were almost Waterloo Black Hawks.

During the Black Hawks’ first decade in the Cedar Valley, the club was operated as a non-profit organization. Community business leaders took a hand in overseeing the team, with some of Waterloo’s most prominent citizens serving as team president. The job changed hands each season. By 1973, the Hawks needed more consistent, year-round management. Seventy-one shareholders put up money, and veteran player Jack Barzee was appointed president and publicity director (as well as still skating as a forward).

Dave Swick was a year removed from retirement as an active player. He and Barzee had been part of Waterloo’s United States Hockey League dynasty during the middle 1960s. From 1963/64 to 1967/68, the Black Hawks won five straight championships. Now the shareholders hoped the new-but-familiar coach could lead the Hawks back to the top of the league, even while Swick continued to spend 40 hours each week as an iron worker. There was no budget for a fulltime head coach in 1973.

“Jack would hunt up players all summer long,” remembers Swick. “Jack would call them, and we would have a big tryout. They came from all over the country…Maybe half our team was already here from the year before, and half would want to do other things. To move up. So we'd have to find five or six good [new] hockey players."

Swick had 40 candidates for the 1973/74 roster when tryouts began in the second week of October. The group included several of Swick's former teammates. Forwards Jim Smith and Chris Batley had been Black Hawks since 1962. So had goaltender Jim Coyle. Defenseman Bud McRae was even Waterloo's player/coach during four of the team's title seasons. Dave Mazur and John Lesyshen were also carryovers from the 60s. More recent arrivals like Dale Pennock and Hal Murphy had already proven themselves during the winter of 1972/73.

Newly aspiring professional players may have brought special optimism to their Waterloo tryouts that fall. The USHL was in initial discussions to become a farm league for the World Hockey Association, as the WHA tried to supplant the NHL as North America's preeminent hockey league. Talks between the USHL and WHA would continue throughout the season, with periodic rumors that an affiliate agreement was just over the horizon.

Waterloo lost two exhibition games against the Des Moines Capitols of the International Hockey League, then won against the Minnesota Junior Stars of the Midwest Junior Hockey League. Swick trimmed more than a dozen prospects from the preseason roster after those early matchups.

Two days prior to an intersquad scrimmage – which would be the basis for Swick's final decisions – Waterloo's coach had some new options to assess.

"The Carlson Brothers showed up at the rink one night, and they had a fella who came with them who said he was their manager," Swick recalls. "Of course, we never heard of a manager for a hockey player where we're playing in Iowa. These kids were just out of high school in Northern Minnesota, and they were good hockey players."

Good enough to stick around and participate in the intersquad game.

On a Saturday night in a mostly empty McElroy Auditorium, 651 fans had the only opportunity to see the Carlsons wear Black Hawks colors. Jack scored in the first period. Steve added a goal in the second. Their red-sweatered squad lost to white-clad opposition 7-5.

* * *

"I couldn't use all three of them," says Swick, now a little more than 50 years later.

That wasn't what the Carlson's well-dressed manager wanted to hear.

"He says, 'No, you gotta use all three, or none.' So we talked, and ordinarily I could have used all three of them, but that year we had a pretty fair team. So I said 'I can use them, but…' and they said 'No, all three, or nobody stays.'"

The Hawks' roster just didn't have room for 20-year-old Jeff, 19-year-old Jack, and 18-year-old Steve Carlson. On an autumn Sunday, Swick wrote out his season-opening roster without the three late arrivals. He also asked Barzee to call an old friend.

Leonard "Oakie" Brumm had overseen a couple of college hockey programs as well as a team of players at Michigan's Marquette Branch Prison. He founded the Des Moines Oak Leafs in 1961, the Black Hawks in 1962, then his hometown Marquette Iron Rangers in 1964. After a season away from coaching, Brumm was returning to lead the Iron Rangers again in 1973.

Ten years earlier, Brumm had brought Swick to Waterloo from the Upper Peninsula.

"I was construction worker. I could see a lot of work in Marquette. I only had played against Oakie, I had never played for him," says Swick. "I used to take my kids to the park every night. We'd been down there running around the park, and I pulled up to a stop sign leaving, and a guy turns the corner and he backs up.

"He says 'Swick?'

"I said, 'Yeah, how you doing?'

"He said, 'I'm Oakie.'

"I said, 'Yeah, I know you're Oakie.'

"He said, 'OK, would you follow me home?'

"I had my wife and the kids in the car, so he said, 'Just follow me.' So when I went to the house he said, 'How would you like go to Waterloo?'

"My wife was in school at the time going to Northern Michigan. I said, 'We're pretty much squared away here.'

"Well he said, 'Go down over the Fourth of July; just see what you think of the town.'

"So I came down and everything went good. I'm a believer, and I'm a Christian, and I think somebody is looking out for me, because next thing you know, I'm sitting in Waterloo. I was going to come for two or three years. I was still in Waterloo when I retired 35 years later."

Despite being just 5-feet, 4-inches, Swick was Waterloo's second-leading scorer in 1963/64. Undersized but feisty, he was a fan favorite, as well as being popular among his teammates. Swick was the Hawks' captain beginning in 1967.

Although Swick only played one season for Brumm, Waterloo's founding coach left an indelible impression.

"Oakie was my type of guy," says Swick.

"One day on the bus, we're headed for Green Bay and we're coming out of Electric Park [near the rink], and the bus stopped. Oakie says to the bus driver, 'What are you doing?'

"The driver said, 'That guy just went by and said 'Wait a minute.''

"[Oakie] said, 'Wait a minute?!? He knows when he should have been here.'

"So [that player] followed us all the way to Green Bay. Oakie said, 'I don't care what he's doing. He better not be late again, or he'll follow us again.' He didn't care who you were or what you were, and I think he gave the impression when he told you something on the ice, he meant it."

Unlike the Black Hawks, the 1973/74 Iron Rangers had a roster which could accommodate keeping the Carlsons together.

"[Jack Barzee] called Oak and said, 'We've got these three kids who are pretty good. I think you'll be able to use them.'

"So we send them up to Marquette, and Oakie thanked me a thousand times. He said they were three of the potential better players. They made his team and drew crowds, because people liked them."

* * *

One week after the red-versus-white scrimmage, the Black Hawks visited Marquette for the second game of a season-opening road trip. The rink there – the Palestra – was an old, unheated venue evoking a barn in more than just hockey slang. In the dead of the Northern Michigan winter, the Iron Rangers would run a construction site heater before the crowd arrived. By order of the fire marshal, it had to be turned off before the doors opened as a safety precaution. The boards at one end of the ice were built just inside a concrete wall, meaning they didn't flex, even with the heaviest body check. Opposing players had to walk through the hostile crowd on the way to the dressing room.

Less than three minutes into the game, Jack Carlson was in the penalty box for elbowing. It was the first of three trips. In the mid-second period Bob Lamoureux scored a power play goal while Carlson was off for roughing. Waterloo added another goal in the third for a 2-0 shutout win.

Three minor penalties may not have accurately captured the sentiment between the Carlsons and their almost-teammates. The Iron Rangers visited McElroy Auditorium the following weekend to extend what the *Waterloo Courier* referred to as the Hawks' "…feud with the Carlson brothers…"

"The Black Hawks charged last week that the Carlson brothers were coming in with their sticks high. They were looking for the same tactics last night and seemed to find what they expected," Russ Smith reported in his November 4th game story.

"Trouble started in earnest 52 seconds into the third period when [Dale] Pennock decked Jack Carlson twice with body checks and Carlson got up the second time swinging with Waterloo's Bob Lamoureux."

Jack Carlson may have been just 19, but his decision not to drop the gloves with the 6-foot, 6-inch, 23-year-old Pennock was astute. Although Waterloo won the game 7-4, it was a productive night for the three brothers. Collectively, they were responsible for two goals, an assist, and 16 penalty minutes.

"That's always the thing that bothers you. You cut a kid and then he turns around and he burns you," says Swick. "The Carlsons were Marquette's whole team, and all they wanted to do was play hockey. Oakie said he had them staying in a basement with three beds in it. He said they were happier than a lark."

A rematch the next day was more measured. Instead of 96 combined penalty minutes, the two teams accumulated just 26. The Carlsons made significant contributions: a goal from Steve, two assists from Jack, and another by Jeff. Waterloo came out on top 5-4 in overtime.

"They were all pretty good scorers. And then of course, Jack was a tough guy," says Swick. "He did what he had to do. Let's put it that way…and the other two were good hockey players who could score. Jack would go in the corner and muscle three or four people [with Jeff and Steve] standing out front waiting for him to get the puck. He'd get it there."

The Carlsons were on the winning side when Waterloo visited Marquette at the end of December. Steve scored a goal in the second period, then assisted on the game-winner in the third as the Iron Rangers prevailed 4-3. During the course of six meetings that season, the Hawks won four times. Steve proved to be the most productive brother during the series, notching eight points (four goals, four assists). Jeff was responsible for six (three goals, three assists), and Jack had four (one goal, three assists).

* * *

In January, Steve Carlson was selected for the USHL All-Star team. Top players from eight USHL clubs played together against – and lost to – the defending champion Thunder Bay Twins. Jack and Jeff Carlson were named honorable mention All Stars.

By the end of the season, Steve was tied for sixth in league scoring with 79 points (34 goals, 45 assists) in 48 games. Jack was eighth in the USHL; his 42 goals and 29 assists added up to 71 points. Marquette finished second in the Northern Division. Waterloo was second in the South. Both teams eventually lost to Thunder Bay in the playoffs: the Iron Rangers in the divisional final and the Hawks in the championship series.

Jack Carlson's goal-scoring and toughness led the league to name him the USHL's Most Valuable Player. That summer, he was drafted 117th overall by the Detroit Red Wings. However, the three brothers elected to stay together a little longer. They signed with the WHA's Minnesota Fighting Saints. A player development agreement between the WHA and USHL never materialized; instead the Carlsons were assigned to the Johnstown Jets.

Jack went on to an impressive NHL career. He debuted with the Minnesota North Stars in 1979. By the time he retired, the middle Carlson had played in 236 regular season games, stacking up 417 penalty minutes. Steve spent most of the 1979/80 season with the Los Angeles Kings. Jeff briefly played in the WHA, spending much of his long career in the minor leagues.

However, their stay in Johnstown, Pennsylvania, made them pop culture icons, at least in the hockey community. That's where the *Slap Shot* script originated. The Carlsons became the Hansons, the Jets became the Chiefs, and legions of fans learned about putting on the foil, Eddie Shore, and capturing the spirit of the thing.

Clearly, *Slap Shot*'s producers got a good deal on those boys.

Swick wasn't overly impressed by the film.

"They didn't go through town mooning people and stuff. I don't think they were that type. That was just something for the movie," Swick reflects. "They were tough, but they didn't fight all the time, like that movie showed. I think they were just some young kids from Northern Minnesota that made it [in hockey]."

Despite cutting the Carlsons, Swick was named the 1973/74 USHL Coach of the Year. He led the Hawks to a pair of runner-up finishes (Thunder Bay won their third consecutive championship, beating Waterloo for a second time in 1975). Swick left the Black Hawks bench in the fall of 1976 but returned to coaching with a long stint leading the Waterloo Warriors high school team.

"I often wondered in my own mind, what could have happened if I would have had room for [the Carlson brothers] to stay in Waterloo," Swick says. "They didn't look like hockey players, but they were good hockey players…If we would have had them here, we might have packed McElroy a few more times."

Hockey in Waterloo – and everywhere else – might never have been the same.

Tragic MVP

This article for waterlooblackhawks.com was posted on October 31, 2024 and laid groundwork for jerseys which the team wore during the following month to benefit the American Cancer Society.

The United States Hockey League of the 1960s was just the place for a player like Elov Seger. As an All-American on college hockey's best team, he had the skills which might have made him a successful professional. However Seger's engineering degree offered better career prospects than the always-uncertain life of a minor leaguer at a time when the NHL had only six teams.

USHL "senior hockey" came to Waterloo in 1962. Elov Seger also arrived that same fall, two weeks before the opening game. Like his teammates, he worked 40 hours during the week, then skated on weekends. Seger was the Black Hawks' Most Valuable Player during the inaugural season. By early 1965, he had helped Waterloo win a pair of league championships. But by March of 1968, Elov Seger was dead. His life was cut short by a brain tumor.

He was three months from his 28th birthday.

* * *

Fort Frances, Ontario, and International Falls, Minnesota, share a bridge across the Rainy River. Small farms, thick forests, and a variety of wetlands surround the otherwise remote cities. The landscape has always attracted hunters and fishermen. Mando – the Minnesota and Ontario Paper Company – operated mills on each side of the river in the mid-20th Century, and the two communities enjoyed a symbiotic, hard-working prosperity across the international border.

Elov Seger was born on the Canadian side in the summer of 1940. He was the youngest of five and the only son in the family. His eldest sister was 18 when he arrived. Seger's father – a Swedish immigrant – died before Elov had turned seven.

Seger was still a pre-teen when the Rainy River area achieved hockey fame across Canada. The local Fort Frances Canadians reached the Allan Cup final in back-to-back years. After a loss in their first attempt, the Canadians won the trophy in 1952, earning distinction as the country's top senior team. The morning after their championship-clinching home win versus the Stratford Indians, newspapers across Canada reported on the passionate support shown by Fort Frances fans:

> Last night, the town was jubilant.
>
> The strong partisan crowd, many of them plaid-clad pulp mill and bush workers had ably supported their team through the final. Some stood in line for hours for tickets and even had meals brought to them.

Seger soon began making his own reputation at the local rink. During the 1956/57 season, he was fast approaching his adult height of six feet, with blond hair trimmed high and tight. Skating for a squad known as the Palcos, Seger and his teammates celebrated the local championship for their age group. When the season was over, area hockey leaders presented him with the community's Calder Trophy as the top juvenile player in Fort Frances.

One sports season led into another, and Seger seemed perpetually in motion. He played basketball, golf, and even badminton with some noteworthy renown. Football was his most prestigious pursuit away from the ice. In 1957, Seger was the quarterback and captain of the Fort Frances Muskies high school squad. He and his teammates would travel across the river to use International Falls Sports Stadium for their most significant home games. In late October, that's where they reversed a long run of success by their rivals from Kenora, winning 26-7 behind Seger's two passing touchdowns and a rushing score. He shared the offensive huddle with Art Berglund, who would eventually make his way into both the U.S. Hockey Hall of Fame and IIHF Hall of Fame. Berglund had a remarkable career as a USA Hockey executive, helping to lead over 30 American national teams into international competition. Those achievements came after he left Fort Frances for hockey stardom at Colorado College.

Like Berglund, Seger was also planning for college south of the border. He was regularly an honor roll student, and – as was customary at that time in Ontario – remained in school for Grade 13, focused on college prep courses. In the spring of 1958, he graduated with 72 classmates. The commencement speaker – a local business leader – admonished the young graduates that the challenges of the era would require them to work harder, while returning to the fundamentals. It was a message that the hockey-playing, 18-year-old Elov Seger must have relished.

* * *

"Hank Akervall and Elov were the two key defensemen for us, and basically they played solid defense," remembered Bob Mikesch more than six decades after he was Seger's Michigan Tech teammate. "Neither one of them were big scoring threats, but they were very good defensively and really passed the puck well. They made the plays you need to make to get out of your own end."

When Seger arrived in Houghton, Michigan, his new school was officially still known as the Michigan College of Mining and Technology. Then – as now – Michigan Tech was regarded as an academically stringent institution. Any student with uncertain math skills was bound to struggle. There were no shortcuts for star hockey players. Seger went to work in the Civil Engineering program.

In that era of college sports, freshmen were not eligible to play varsity games. Seger and his classmates were relegated to the freshmen squad. The 1958/59 Huskies frosh team went undefeated, showing great promise for a program which was already earning strong results. The varsity was a solid 16-10-1 that winter under third-year head coach John MacInnes.

A Toronto native, MacInnes was well-positioned for success as an NCAA coach. He had been a goaltender at the University of Michigan and played professionally in the International Hockey League. More importantly, he had strong Canadian recruiting connections. At the time, Canadian collegians dominated the sport, particularly at schools in the Midwest and Colorado. For example, when Seger was a sophomore, the Huskies were runners-up for the 1960 NCAA title, falling to Denver in the national championship game. The Pioneers only had one American on their roster. Michigan Tech had two. That spring, some college coaches advocated a ban on recruiting Canadian junior players.

The remoteness of Houghton, Michigan, was sometimes a more practical recruiting and travel obstacle. For Seger, the woodsy Keweenaw Peninsula likely felt reminiscent of Fort Frances. It may have been a much different experience for teammates imported from Toronto and more urban settings.

"Getting in and out sometimes would be a challenge," confirmed Mikesch. "Most of the time we went by bus. But if you were going to fly out of here, you'd have to plan on leaving at least one day in advance, because you could never rely on the weather."

A Huskies' bus trip from Houghton to Ann Arbor was over 500 miles. It was actually a shorter ride to play the University of North Dakota in Grand Forks. Life on campus was rugged in some ways but came with other compensations for Michigan Tech players.

"They lived in barracks, old army barracks that were behind Michigan Tech," said Mikesch, who himself commuted to campus from his nearby home in Hancock, Michigan. "Of course [the players] being old enough to drink and everything...They weren't allowed to do too much drinking in public during hockey season, but they used to have a lot of good times."

In 1959/60, the Huskies finished 21-10-1. They had beaten Denver in three of four meetings before falling in the national title game. Seger eased his way into the lineup. As one of four sophomore defensemen, he played in just over half of Tech's games.

The 1960/61 campaign was an off year for the program. Top scorer Paul Coppo had graduated. He was on the way to the Green Bay Bobcats, and eventually the U.S. Hockey Hall of Fame. Seger earned more ice time, but Michigan Tech finished 16-13-0.

Seger was never destined to be a centerpiece of the offense, but he had learned a lot in three years on campus. He played in every game during Michigan Tech's 1961/62 NCAA Championship season, serving as an alternate captain and bringing a steady presence to the blue line. One measure of his success that winter: when the Huskies created a "Most Improved Player" team award later in the decade, they named it in Seger's honor.

Michigan Tech lost the first two games of the season during a trip to visit their rivals from the University of Michigan. A month later in Houghton, the Wolverines prevailed again, 4-2. Tech would not lose another game during the remainder of the season. Their January 6th victory in a rematch against Michigan was the beginning of a 21-game winning streak which carried all the way to Utica, New York, the site for that year's four-team NCAA Tournament.

One of the most important wins during the streak came in Ann Arbor during a crucial fifth meeting with the Wolverines. It was the championship game of the Western Collegiate Hockey Association Tournament on March 3rd. The 6-4 result assured Tech's bid into the National Semifinals.

Wolverine supporters must have been confident early. Described as "a record University of Michigan crowd of 3,882," the home fans cheered their team to a 2-0 lead, but two Huskies goals in the last minute before intermission sent the two sides to their dressing rooms with a tie score. The Wolverines retook the lead with the only goal in the second period. However, Seger scored to re-tie the matchup in the third. Tech wouldn't trail again. They took their first lead 13 seconds later, then got the goal which proved to be the winner with 7:25 to go in regulation.

Besides Tech, Michigan was also invited to the national tournament. Clarkson and St. Lawrence were waiting in Utica for the western schools two weeks later. The weekend began with a stunning upset; Clarkson edged the Wolverines, 5-4.

"They did a hell of a favor for us," admitted Mikesch. "We beat Michigan that year – twice – but that was unusual. Michigan generally was one of the top teams to beat."

In the other semifinal, Michigan Tech easily coasted past St. Lawrence 6-1. The championship matchup against Clarkson was just as one-sided: Huskies 7, Golden Knights 1. Tech scored early, led the entire night, and broke the game open during a one-sided third period. Seger and Akervall were both chosen for the All-Tournament First Team along with Huskies forwards Lou Angotti and John Ivanitz.

"They had a huge, huge gathering at the airport when we flew back into town," said Mikesch, remembering the estimated 1,500 fans waiting to celebrate when the Huskies emerged from their plane. "Yeah, we got treated like kings."

Seger was an All-American, one of four Tech players to be chosen for that honor by the American Hockey Coaches Association. He finished his college career with six goals and 20 assists in 72 games. Three months later, Seger also wrapped up his academic career, successfully earning his Civil Engineering degree within four years. The graduation ceremony was three days after he had turned 22.

* * *

Leonard "Oakie" Brumm was the hockey equivalent of Johnny Appleseed. He planted teams at seemingly every stop during his long association with the sport. In 1962, he came to Waterloo.

That summer, a major renovation of Waterloo Auditorium on the National Cattle Congress grounds had included a new floor and ice-making equipment. The versatile old building was ready to welcome a new team. Launching new clubs was Brumm's specialty. A year earlier, he helped establish the Des Moines Oak Leafs. The Marquette, Michigan, native had worked everywhere from his Upper Peninsula hometown to Alaska. In Waterloo, he would simultaneously be a defenseman and the head coach, plus taking the added responsibility of building the first Black Hawks roster.

With Brumm's roots in the U.P., a vast number of people could have tipped him off about Elov Seger's exploits at Michigan Tech. Brumm might have heard directly from Huskies Coach John MacInnes; a dozen years earlier, Brumm and MacInnes had been teammates at the University of Michigan. Or perhaps Seger just found his way to Waterloo because it's where everyone else from the Rainy River area seemed to be going. Reportedly as many as a dozen skaters from Fort Frances, International Falls, and nearby communities tried out for the Black Hawks in 1962. In addition to Seger, Brian Latta, Dan Dillworth, and Don Millette all made the roster.

Regina, Saskatchewan, native Don "Butch" Leskun also came south to join a Waterloo roster filled with new arrivals.

"We had to have a place to stay," Leskun remembered, "And we always said, 'Oh, we're staying at the Hotel Yumka,' and they'd say 'Where the heck is that?'

"And I said, 'Well, it's on the river there.' Then finally, we'd have to tell them it's the YMCA. We did little things like that and got to know each other. We became a really good family because of how we met and the type of people that Oakie Brumm accumulated there. We all became pretty good friends."

It didn't take long for Leskun to appreciate Seger, both as a friend and a teammate.

"He was a kind of a lumbering, big, nice guy," said Leskun. "You know, he'd never get into fights. He was good. You could never get around him, because he was tall, and he had a good reach, but he never really roughed it up. He just was a good hockey player."

The Hawks lost their debut game on November 17, 1962, falling at home against the Rochester Mustangs 6-2. A rematch the next night was closer, but Rochester came out on top again.

A week later in Des Moines, the Hawks played a back-and-forth game against the Oak Leafs. Just less than three minutes were left when Seger and Leskun set up the first game-winning goal in Black Hawks history. Brian Latta scored it, and then added another seconds later, to lift Waterloo to a 7-5 victory.

Waterloo defeated Des Moines again a few nights later for the team's first home win. The Hawks spent the entire season right near .500, rarely above that mark but never more than a couple of games below. They had some of their best results in February, then lost four of their last five as the season ended in early March. At 16-16-0, Waterloo placed third in the five-team USHL.

A middling record was still good enough for local fans to embrace the team.

"The people of the town all invited us for dinners all the time or Thanksgiving and Christmas," said Leskun. "You know, they took to us."

Seger finished the season with four goals and 15 assists. On March 10th – the final night on the home schedule – Team President Bob Keller presented Seger with the Black Hawks Most Valuable Player award at intermission. The recognition included a trophy and a letterman-style jacket. To make the selection, team leaders polled local media, as well as opposing USHL coaches. Seger had made a strong first impression, and the next fall the game program described him as a player who "...excels at taking his man out of the play, retrieving the puck, and starting a break out play..."

That offseason, Seger was a regular on Waterloo's golf courses. He and Leskun became members at Sunnyside Country Club. In August, they both entered the Waterloo Open. Seger shot an 80 during the amateur competition, five strokes away from the chance to play with the pros on Sunday. The summer was even more eventful in Seger's personal life as he courted Diane Steen, a local girl who worked for the *Waterloo Courier*. The couple had a late September wedding in Zion Lutheran Church on the city's west side.

Seger also settled into his fulltime job working for Waterloo Steel & Equipment. His engineering talents were well-utilized, including for one feature of Waterloo's multistory downtown parking ramp, which Leskun remembered.

"[There was] a galvanized chute where they would put snow and push it down onto a truck, and you'd see [the chute] hanging on the side of the building. I don't know if it's still there or not, but he designed that, and he was pretty proud of that...[He] always said 'See, that chute? I designed that.'"

Wayne Wirkkula – who later became one of Seger's Waterloo teammates – noted Seger's willingness to share his math skills with his Waterloo Steel coworkers.

"Those people that ran that company, they loved him," said Wirkkula. "He would work with some of the manufacturing people and was teaching them algebra and all kinds of stuff like that. Elov had personality and intelligence, very smart...And you couldn't ruffle him in any way. He would have a smile and [just was] a good, pleasant guy."

When the 1963/64 hockey schedule began, the Black Hawks struggled during their early games. However, Waterloo began winning consistently over the weekend after Thanksgiving. That included defeating the U.S. Olympic team during an exhibition matchup in early December. Seger tallied an assist on a third period goal which kept Waterloo out of reach.

By mid-February, the Hawks were 17-8-0 and in position to earn at least a share of the USHL championship in just their second season. Half of Waterloo's losses had been against the Green Bay Bobcats. Green Bay visited on February 16th and Seger did his part to help secure a share of the title. His three assists helped Waterloo build a big lead and weather a four-goal Bobcat comeback. The Hawks finally prevailed 7-6 in overtime in front of 4,855 relieved home fans.

That 1963/64 season had included more steady play from Seger. He scored four goals and set up 22 others. In March, he even added a goal during a 4-3 non-league matchup versus the Cincinnati Wings, the Central Professional Hockey League affiliate of the Detroit Red Wings.

Yet, the Black Hawks' success did not prevent significant offseason changes. Brumm left Waterloo. He returned to Marquette where he would establish another new USHL team, the Iron Rangers. Bud McRae became head coach. McRae had joined the Hawks in 1963/64 and made substantial contributions to the championship season. In the autumn of 1964, Waterloo also added veteran Bill Dobbyn, already illustrious as a professional skater in North America and Europe.

McRae, Dobbyn, and Bernie Nielsen were each excellent defensemen, and with Seger, Waterloo was loaded on the blue line for 1964/65. However, depth at forward was a problem, especially in the absence of Tim Taylor, who was called away at midseason to join the U.S. National Team for the IIHF World Championships. By New Year's Day, Waterloo was just 2-7-0. It was a situation which called for creativity; McRae's solution was to make Seger a centerman.

"Elov was an extremely good stick handler and puck controller, and saw the ice…[He was] just a very, very good hockey player for our league," said Wirkkula. "That opening developed at center, and Elov went along with it. He liked to carry the puck and he did very well at center. We won the championship again that year."

Waterloo began to roll and earned a 7-2-0 record in January. During the final weekend of that month, the Hawks battled for a crucial weekend sweep of the league-leading St. Paul Steers. Seger scored goals in each of the two wins. He added more timely points in February, and the Hawks kept winning.

Waterloo needed all the victories and all the scoring they could manage to stage a remarkable comeback. By winning 10 of their last 12 games, the Hawks edged the Steers for the USHL title. An imbalanced number of games meant the race came down to winning percentage, with Waterloo at .607 (17-11-0) and St. Paul at .577 (15-11-0). Had the Hawks lost one of their January matchups against St. Paul, the championship would have flipped to the Steers. Playing much of the season away from his natural position, Seger tallied five goals and nine assists. Dating back to his senior season at Michigan Tech, the 25-year-old had been part of three championship teams in four years.

Nonetheless, within three months of Waterloo's last 1964/65 game, Elov and Diane Seger were new residents of Rochester, Minnesota.

* * *

"Definitely he wanted to play defense," said Wayne Wirkkula, explaining Seger's abrupt northward relocation and eventual reemergence as a member of the Rochester Mustangs. "And he knew a lot of those guys. He'd played against a lot of the [Bill] Reichart's and those guys…[Tom] Yurkovich…those guys up there were at North Dakota, Minnesota, Michigan Tech, the Western Collegiate Hockey League, so he knew a lot of those guys."

Lou Nanne was one of the WCHA alumni playing for Rochester. As a Minnesota Gopher, he had met Seger's Michigan Tech teams, then faced him during subsequent seasons in Waterloo. Six decades later, Nanne had a few lasting impressions of the big defenseman.

"I remember playing against him," Nanne said. "First of all, he was a real nice guy and a very, very solid player…He knew his position well. He was tough to beat defensively. He was very, very consistent."

Nanne and Seger were Rochester teammates for two seasons. However, they didn't have as many opportunities to become acquainted as players in Waterloo. Nanne was part of a commuting contingent who traveled in from Minneapolis, carpooling to games and practices along with approximately half of the Mustangs roster. The rest of the team – including Seger – were fulltime Rochester residents. The Mustangs had been American senior hockey's dominant team during the 1950s, and the city's enthusiastic hockey community embraced the club.

"It's a wonderful city. You know, at that time, we were less than 45,000 people. Now they're over 100,000," said Nanne. "You had a great city…a city of means. So, it was great living conditions, and good players would come there, because [Rochester] could afford to run a good program. But the most important thing was the jobs that [players] could get."

IBM was one of the prominent employers. International Business Machines was perhaps the premier technology company of the era. Their employee roster included the Mustangs' talented goalie Yurkovich, their scoring star Reichart, player/coach Bert Aikens, and others. With Seger's math and engineering background, he was a natural fit. In Rochester, he was also reunited with at least one Fort Frances native, Dick Carpenter, and a Michigan Tech teammate, Gene Rebellato.

On game nights, the Mustangs came together to skate in one of the smallest rinks around: Mayo Civic Auditorium. It was considerably shorter than most ice sheets, including a building like Waterloo Auditorium (later renamed McElroy Auditorium). In fact, the neutral zone in Rochester was so skinny that there wasn't enough room to include a center red line.

Nanne admitted that the tight confines created challenges.

"We had the worst rink in the league, but we'd sell out. It was a very physical place to play, because there's no room for anybody to operate. You know, you're always seeing bodies."

Waterloo tended to play better than most teams traveling to Civic Auditorium. The first time they visited Seger and the Mustangs in 1965/66, the Hawks came away with a 6-4 victory. Although Waterloo eventually claimed their third straight championship that season, the clubs split six head-to-head games. Seger played in each meeting, notching one assist.

"There were never any hard feelings or anything like that," noted Leskun. "You joke around. If he happened to hit you, you'd say 'Geez, Seeg, you do that one more time, I'm gonna deck you,' and he'd just laugh."

After the regular season, Seger made an unexpected trip back to Waterloo for a special game against the Hawks. In early April, the USHL staged a benefit for St. Paul goaltender Bill Halbrehder, who had lost an eye as the result of an accident in practice. Seger was a late addition to the visiting All-Star team, replacing Green Bay's Carl Lackey. Waterloo topped the USHL's best 7-4, and the game raised over $2,300 for Halbrehder.

Less than two years later, fans at McElroy Auditorium were taking up a collection for Seger.

He played through the 1966/67 season, but by the summer of 1967, something was clearly wrong. Living in Rochester, Seger had access to some of the best medical specialists in the world. By August, they had discovered a formidable brain tumor. At age 27 – married for less than four years and father to a young daughter – Seger had major surgery at St. Mary's Hospital on the Mayo Clinic campus.

He would rarely leave the hospital in the months before his family, teammates, and fans lost him on March 8, 1968.

* * *

On the Sunday of Seger's funeral in Rochester, the Black Hawks and Mustangs were on a bus together, headed for the Lake Superior shore. The two teams drove halfway across Minnesota for a Sunday exhibition in anticipation of Duluth joining the USHL the following season. Seger's service at Rochester's Congregational Church was winding down around the same time warm-ups were beginning at Duluth Auditorium. Butch Leskun and Tom Yurkovich missed the game and attended the funeral as pallbearers.

"My wife and I went up and saw him in the hospital, and then the next time we went was for the funeral," said Leskun.

Seger had been the best man when Don and Nancy Leskun were married in 1964. The Segers and the Leskuns, and the Black Hawks and the Mustangs couldn't have anticipated how quickly Elov Seger's illness would take him away.

Star athlete. Talented, hard-working employee. Big likeable guy. Gone in less than nine fleeting, yet agonizing months.

"I think he could have gone pro, if he was a meaner guy," said Wayne Wirkkula. "Everybody respected him, and he had the size where nobody was going to bother him, but he just played the game, played it extremely smart."

Two days after his funeral in Rochester, Seger was buried in Fort Frances.

He might have played a few more seasons in the USHL. His engineering career might have lasted into the 1990s or even the early 21st century. He might still be with us today to tell his own story.

"Elov was kind of a quiet, gentle giant…a really, really, really nice guy," said Bob Mikesch.

He was three months from his 28th birthday. A lot of people would have liked nothing more than to celebrate that birthday – and many more – with him.

Waterloo's First All-Star Game

This story was written for the Black Hawks' 2009/10 yearbook.

Officially, there was only one All-Star team at McElroy Auditorium on April 2, 1966, but the 1965/66 Black Hawks were a solid squad on their own, as they proved in a 7-4 win against the best of the United States Hockey League. In March of that season, Waterloo had earned their third consecutive USHL title. A victory against the league's top talent, pooled together, was a final accolade and an impressive feat.

"There were only six teams in the NHL at that time," remembered St. Paul Steers goalie Bill Halbrehder, "so there were some excellent players who were not quite at the NHL level, but wanted to play competitive hockey."

However the game wasn't scheduled just so the Hawks and their fans could feel a little more pride in a season full of accomplishments. The inspiration for the matchup pitting the champs against the All-Stars was a late-season accident, which ended Halbrehder's career.

The young goalie was a rookie for St. Paul. Originally from Superior, Wisconsin, Halbrehder had finished playing at the University of Minnesota-Duluth the previous winter, and, like many USHLers of the era, was taking advantage of the opportunity the league offered to continue playing at a high level. As a Bulldog, Halbrehder had started for three seasons. During his senior year, he helped UMD to one of two winning campaigns during the 1960s. In a 6-5 overtime loss to the Michigan Wolverines in 1964, he had made a then-NCAA-record 77 saves. The mark still stands as a Minnesota-Duluth all-time best.

Green Bay Gambler assistant coach Carl Lackey, who played against Halbrehder while at Michigan State and then in the USHL as a member of the Marquette Iron Rangers, recalled that Halbrehder's personality came across in his play.

"He was a very good hockey player, very competitive," said Lackey. "He was a good guy."

Lackey was one of the players selected for the USHL All-Star squad, but could not make it to McElroy Auditorium for the Halbrehder Benefit Game. The players who were on the ice, on both benches, played for free, as did the officials. Ticket receipts went to Halbrehder who had lost his left eye in a practice accident a few weeks earlier.

"We were practicing for the playoffs and scrimmaging the Rochester Mustangs," says Halbrehder. "A Rochester player came in on a breakaway with one of my defensemen chasing him. All three of us collided at the net."

In the pile-up a skate clipped Halbrehder's form-fitting goalie mask and lacerated his eye. The injury was severe enough for doctors to remove the eye at the hospital that night. A week later, bandaged but back on his feet, Halbrehder suited up for the Steers' team picture.

"It was the last time I put on the pads," he says.

League officials and players built up momentum for holding an All-Star game to help Halbrehder with medical expenses and the adjustment to his new challenge.

"That was a very unusual thing to do," says Lackey. "Whoever came up with the idea was really ahead of the game."

The Black Hawks fielded a team to meet the All-Stars which represented the nucleus of five straight championships. Player-coach Bud McRae led a defense which included Bill Dobbyn, Wayne Wirkkula, and Bernie Nielsen. Future Yale Head Coach Tim Taylor, along with longtime Hawks Jim Smith, Jack Barzee, and Dave Swick were among the forwards. The foundation of the 60's Black Hawks, goalies Jim Coyle and Terry Hoath, both played in the game.

Rochester Mustangs goalie Tom Yurkovich, later the USHL's Referee-in-Chief, was in the crease for the All-Stars. Wayne McQuaig and Bob Cox represented Marquette. Paul Coppo and John Mayasich were there from the Green Bay Bobcats. Two of Halbrehder's St. Paul teammates, with names almost any hockey fan would recognize, also skated at McElroy that night.

Bill Masterton played with, and coached, the All-Star team. Like Lackey and Halbrehder, Masterton had been a star in the NCAA, playing for the University of Denver Pioneers. He was an All-American there and the Most Valuable Player of the 1961 college hockey tournament, one of three which the Pioneers won during his time in Denver. Masterton's chances of making the NHL appeared to be over by the middle 1960's, but when the Minnesota North Stars joined the league just a few seasons after Bill Halbrehder's benefit game, Masterton earned a spot on their roster. Halfway through the inaugural season, in a game against the Oakland Seals, Masterton was knocked backwards into the dasherboards, leaving him unconscious. He never woke up and died in the hospital two days later at age 29.

"Besides Bill's outstanding hockey skills," remembers Halbrehder, "he was an absolute gentleman. I don't think I ever heard a harsh word out of him, which was rare for a hockey locker room."

The NHL would create the Bill Masterton Trophy to honor his memory later that year. The award is still handed out after each season by the Professional Hockey Writers Association to a player exhibiting "...to a high degree, the qualities of perseverance, sportsmanship, and dedication to hockey."

The other notable All-Star that night starred during the defining act of United States hockey history. Herb Brooks skated for the Minnesota Gophers before taking over as the program's Head Coach in 1972, following his USHL playing days. Brooks brought Minnesota to championship heights as a coach, winning three NCAA titles. He caught the attention of U.S. Olympic officials, leading to his opportunity to pilot the 1980 U.S. Olympic team. The "Miracle on Ice" victory over the Soviet Union, the gold medal, and Lake Placid chants of "U-S-A, U-S-A" will forever be attached to the memory of Herb Brooks. His career coaching the New York Rangers, Minnesota North Stars, New Jersey Devils, and Pittsburgh Penguins, and even his posthumous induction into the Hockey Hall of Fame in 2006 could not match the impressive height of what many consider to be the greatest moment in sports history.

While sometimes depicted as hard-driving and difficult to approach, Halbrehder has a different memory of his former teammate.

"Herb became a good friend. He had a great sense of humor and liked to share stories and jokes. He was a beautiful skater and had a great, creative mind for the game, even as a player."

But at McElroy Auditorium, Brooks, Masterton, and the USHL's other notables couldn't equal the Black Hawks. Coyle and Hoath shined in net, combining to stop 37 of 41 All-Star shots. Masterton scored late in the second period, but only after Waterloo had pushed to a 4-0 lead. Taylor and Chris Batley each had a pair of goals on the night for the Hawks.

More importantly, the 2,286 fans in attendance raised $2,361.70 for Halbrehder who says he doesn't remember much about the game itself as he looks over a stick signed for him by many of the participants.

"It was special to have all those guys together and be able to greet them. I was pretty down, as I remember, knowing that my playing days were over. It was one of the best years of hockey I can remember...we were all playing because we loved the game."

Lackey also remembers with affection the era when players were coming from college, rather than trying to get there through the USHL.

"It was the best league in the U.S.A at the time. We wanted to play hockey but also work in our fields. Everybody respected each other and we played good, clean, competitive games."

Although Halbrehder didn't play again, he wasn't done with hockey. Like Lackey, he would become a high school teacher and coach. A P.E. teacher at North St. Paul High, and later the school's Athletic Director, Halbrehder first coached the Polars' boy's team, and later the girl's squad. His most notable former player is probably 17-year NHL veteran Bret Hedican. A Stanley Cup winner with the Carolina Hurricanes in 2006, Hedican was Carolina's nominee for the Masterton trophy that season after coming back from two knee operations and surgery on his back.

During 31 years at North St. Paul, Halbrehder says that having many of his former players in the coaching ranks now is one of the most satisfying legacies from his time in the game.

"I missed playing a lot, but I don't think I was ever bitter about the loss of my eye," he says. "I had a great love for the game, and more than anything, I tried to preach and teach that love of the game to my players."

Perhaps the most prophetic outcome of the 1966 Black Hawks-versus-All-Stars game, which represented the intersection of so many notable players, was a single sentence in a letter Halbrehder sent thanking Black Hawks management for staging the benefit.

According to the *Waterloo Courier*, Halbrehder wrote, "Hockey has done so much for me, that I can hold no regrets at my misfortune."

The game would continue to sustain the once-promising goalie, and four decades later Halbrehder sounds like a man with nothing to regret.

Olympic Tune-Ups

On February 10, 2022, waterlooblackhawks.com presented this story as the Winter Olympics were being staged in Beijing.

The 2022 Olympic Men's Hockey Tournament is officially underway. The first game for the United States will be tomorrow morning (Central Time) against China. Even without NHL stars in this year's competition, the process of choosing the team that represents the United States is much different today than at earlier times.

In 2022, the best available players were brought together from their colleges or international pro clubs with just a matter of weeks' notice. Five or six decades ago, the national team would travel the country (and often beyond) playing exhibition games to both prepare for the Olympics and assess the players competing for a spot on the final roster. For good measure, the pre-Olympic tour was also often a source of funding to help send the national team across the globe to Europe or Asia.

During the 1960s and 70s, the Black Hawks were a "senior" team, with a roster of post-college-aged players. Along with the USHL's other clubs in Green Bay, Rochester, Marquette, and elsewhere, the league was occasionally the source of Olympic talent. It was also a competitive proving ground for the U.S. squads which hoped to bring back a medal.

Ahead of the 1964, 1968, 1972, and 1976 Winter Games, Waterloo hosted the future Olympic team, and saw some memorable exhibitions.

December 8, 1963
Black Hawks 6, USMNT 5

Player/coach Oakie Brumm's jubilant response to Waterloo's first test against a U.S. Olympic Team captured the celebratory mood at Waterloo Auditorium: "I wish I had a jug, I'd have a drink! I don't drink or smoke during the hockey season, but this is an exception."

In Waterloo's second season, and only four years from Team USA winning gold during the 1960 Squaw Valley games, Brumm's "exception" was certainly justified. *Waterloo Courier* writer Burke Evans described the Sunday afternoon 6-5 Black Hawks victory as "…the finest hockey game ever played in Waterloo."

At 11:49 of the first period, Duke Dutkowski finished Mike White's setup that had originated behind the net. The goal broke a 1-1 tie, and Waterloo would lead the rest of the way, thanks in part to four total goals in the opening 20 minutes. Tim Taylor assisted on the last of those scores, on what must have been a particularly satisfying day. Taylor – later the longtime head coach at Yale and eventually head coach of the 1994 U.S. Olympic squad – had just been released from the National Team weeks earlier in mid-November.

It was also a notable day for Bud McRae and Gerry Marttila, who recorded two goals apiece. Paul Johnson also had two goals, but the future Black Hawks scoring ace was playing for the visitors. Johnson – whose #11 was retired by the Black Hawks in 2002, around the time he was inducted into the United States Hockey Hall of Fame – was on his way to his second Olympic tournament. His tally with 1:58 to go set up a thrilling finish, and Waterloo held on behind Jim Coyle's 24 saves. Johnson would join the Hawks fulltime beginning in 1965.

December 9 & 10, 1967
USMNT 8, Black Hawks 1 & USMNT 7, Black Hawks 6

Almost exactly four years later, the National Team tour included a two-night stop in Waterloo. Team USA dominated a Saturday night contest, scoring five times in the second period during the 8-1 victory. Doug Volmar had a hat trick in that period alone. After playing in the Olympics, Volmar would go on to make it briefly to an expanding National Hockey League, playing for the Detroit Red Wings and Los Angeles Kings. Herb Brooks assisted on Volmar's third goal.

The Hawks were much sharper in the nip-and-tuck rematch. Dave Mazur had a hat trick for Waterloo and Paul Johnson scored twice – this time FOR the Hawks – but the National Team stayed out of reach, ultimately leading from 8:08 of the first period, when they scored the opening goal, until the end of the game.

The Hawks were left to wonder what might have happened in overtime, if not for a strange second period score for Team USA. Player/coach Bud McRae described what happened after goalie Jim Coyle snagged a shot: "He caught it and dropped it back over the net. Then it caught in the folds of the net, and when someone tipped the net to get it out, it fell through a hole in the net and the goal judge called it a goal."

Despite that apparent bad break, Waterloo had a chance to tie the score in the closing seconds. Keith Christiansen had already blasted in a Hawks goal from long distance in the second period. Late in the third, he dodged traffic in the offensive zone and was barely denied from close range by goalie Pat Rupp on Waterloo's last best chance.

The next time Waterloo met a group of future American Olympians, Christiansen would be wearing red, white, and blue for the opposing team.

October 29 & 30, 1971
USMNT 10, Black Hawks 2 & USMNT 15, Black Hawks 1

The 1972 U.S. Olympic squad didn't win gold like their 1960 or 1980 counterparts. They did bring back silver medals from Sapporo, Japan, at a time when the Soviet Union was dominant and Czechoslovakia was on the rise.

The American team was good enough to compete with those two hockey powers and more than good enough to hold the Black Hawks at arm's length. Yet going into the third period of the Friday contest – Waterloo's first appearance at McElroy Auditorium during the 1971/72 season – it was just a 2-1 score. The difference at that point in the game was a first period rebound finish from young Robbie Ftorek, assisted by Charlie Brown. Ftorek was just 19 at the time; he would be in the National Hockey League the following season. Meanwhile, Brown would find his way to Waterloo during the years which followed, earning USHL All-Star honors, as well as two league Defenseman of the Year awards.

When that Friday game opened up in the last 20 minutes, the Hawks couldn't keep pace, falling 10-2. Dave Swick scored both Waterloo goals, the last of them with just seconds to play.

Unlike the Friday tilt, the Saturday rematch was never close. Instead of being within a goal at the second intermission, the Hawks trailed 10-1, eventually losing 15-1, the most lopsided defeat in team history up to that time. Of the 25 goals the National Team would score during the weekend, Keith Christiansen – now enshrined in the U.S. Hockey Hall of Fame – scored two and assisted on six others. Brown had two goals and four assists, while Ftorek notched five points.

December 13, 1975
USMNT 6, Black Hawks 3

The final game between the Black Hawks and a U.S. Olympic Team is a story of "almosts," starting in goal. Like Tim Taylor in 1963, Dan Griffin had hoped his time touring with the Nationals would lead to an opportunity to go to Austria (by coincidence, the host nation in both 1964 and 1976).

Also like Taylor, Griffin's Olympic dream deflated just as the winter holidays were arriving.

Joining the Black Hawks in early December, he earned a 3-0, 30-save shutout during his Waterloo debut against the Sioux City Musketeers. Griffin's appearance the next weekend versus his former National Team compatriots didn't go so smoothly. He was on the hook for three goals from 19 first period shots, then gave up the eventual game-winner in the second before a planned goalie swap in the Hawks crease. Better days awaited: spending that lone season in Waterloo, Griffin was ultimately recognized as the Hawks' MVP in the spring.

Meanwhile, Mike Randolph had previously won a pair of Hawks MVP awards. He hoped to turn his USHL success into a spot on the Olympic roster and assisted on one of the goals which had the National Team ahead 3-2 at intermission. Unfortunately, Randolph was not awarded a plane ticket to Innsbruck. Despite the disappointment, he would later call the time he spent with Team USA the best part of his playing career before a legendary high school coaching tenure at Duluth East.

Defenseman Tom Machowski was also skating for the Olympic team that December day, assisting on a third period goal which helped the visitors extend their lead on the way to a 6-3 result. The former Atlanta Flames draft pick was hoping Bob Johnson – his college coach at Wisconsin during the four prior seasons – would include him on the final National Team roster. It was not to be; instead Machowski would join the Hawks later that season and remain in Waterloo into the transitional years as the USHL morphed into a junior hockey league.

The U.S. win against Waterloo moved their tour record to 31-10-2. However, at the Winter Games, Team USA finished fifth, setting the clock turning toward Herb Brooks' all-college 1980 Olympic roster and the Miracle on Ice.

Russia in Retrospect

Five Years After the Black Hawks Went to Omsk

This reflection on the 2012 Junior Club World Cup was the cover story for the 2017 Preseason edition of Hawk Tawk Mag-e-Zine.

The always-complicated relationship between Russia and the United States has experienced changes which would have been nearly impossible to predict five years ago.

Russia's annexation of Crimea and support of Ukrainian separatists has increased tensions with America and western Europe. Alleged interference by Russian hackers in the 2016 U.S. election has led to distrust at a level not seen since the collapse of the Soviet Union. President Donald Trump's alternatively warm-then-frosty statements about Russia and its president, Vladimir Putin, contribute to even more uncertainty about how two of the world's most important countries will deal with each other going into the future.

Just five years ago this month, the Waterloo Black Hawks were involved in on-ice diplomacy with their own Russian counterparts, as well as teams from several other nations during the 2012 Junior Club World Cup in the Siberian city of Omsk.

"As the Hawks' captain I had the privilege of being able to converse with the other captains participating in the tournament," remembered defenseman Ian McCoshen, adding, "The majority of them wanted to communicate…in English, but it was so difficult to truly get a feel for what they were really trying to say."

On Sunday, August 12, 2012, a traveling party of nearly 40 left Waterloo for Moscow, via Chicago and Zurich. Between travel, time zone changes, and traffic, the team did not arrive at their hotel until late Monday.

"It seemed like an eternity until we got there," conceded McCoshen about the drive from the airport, which lasted over two hours and took the Hawks past luxury car dealerships, nuclear power stations, rundown Soviet-era buildings, and billboards for the newest, most exotic electronics, fashion, and consumer goods.

The traveling party would see the city's more resplendent sites on a tour the following evening.

"The architecture in Moscow was jaw dropping, especially around Red Square," said goaltender Eamon McAdam. "Everywhere you looked there was a massive church or building with an elaborate design and paint."

"The buildings we got to see were pretty awesome," added forward Ryan Papa. "While we weren't allowed to go in some of them, just seeing the history behind them and the architecture was unreal. I wish we had a few more days to see that city, but we had bigger things to do."

The Hawks split two exhibition games in Moscow against Russian opponents CSKA and HC MVD – sharing a meal with the latter club before flying over three more time zones, literally to the other side of the world.

Omsk, the host city for the Junior Club World Cup, is among the largest metropolitan areas in the country; players and staff quickly found a few regular haunts around the Ibis Sibir Omsk Hotel.

"We had the freedom to walk outside of our hotel and explore the city a little bit without our translator and tour guide," said McCoshen. "We would venture off to a local coffee shop that was phenomenal and a little pizza place that would remind us of home, as well."

"We had lots of free time to walk around the downtown area and eat at some local restaurants," agreed Papa, adding, "We fell in love with a little café down the street called Berlin Café."

Although thin-crust pizza became a staple and steaks at the Irish-themed Kolchak Restaurant were a welcome luxury, other food and beverage options represented an intense degree of culture shock.

"I am probably not the only one, but I lost a lot of weight because I could not physically force myself to eat some of the food provided, or I simply got sick of eating pasta with ketchup and mayo mixed together…there was no marina sauce, or any sauce for that matter," McCoshen noted.

"We didn't have too many cold drinks while we were there," said Papa, because the team was under orders not to drink the water, and iced beverages were almost nonexistent.

The only ice which really mattered was at Omsk Arena. Waterloo was part of a pool of five teams with clubs representing Belarus, Russia, Czech Republic, and Norway. One week after beginning their journey, McAdam's 27-save effort was the foundation for a 5-0 victory over HC Energie, the Czech representatives. It was the first of several strong performances for the second-year netminder.

"I think that the exposure I got to professional scouts during the trip really helped get my name out there and boosted my stock with the NHL draft," McAdam said. "It was one of the key reasons I got drafted."

Papa's superb offensive play also made a strong impression on the local fans.

"The Facebook requests kept pouring in," he said, "not just for myself but for my teammates as well. One thing that sticks out was how the announcers and the newspapers loved my last name…The support we gained quickly from the fans was awesome. It did not take long before we saw American flags in the arena during games."

Yet that support evaporated – at least temporarily – days later. Both Waterloo and the host Omsk Hawks lost early games against Belarus' Dynamo Shinnik, setting up a winner-take-all pool play finale between the U.S. and Russian entries.

According to McAdam, "My biggest memory of the whole tournament was skating out into the rink where we were playing the Russians and the building was packed. It was a raucous atmosphere and it was one of the loudest, most fun buildings I had played in to date."

Papa scored twice in the 7-3 win – a game which was 4-3 until the final two minutes – while McCoshen contributed an assist and McAdam made 28 saves in front of the 8,573 opposing fans. Justin Kloos also had two goals, including the game winner.

Just 48 hours later, Waterloo was playing another survival game in the semifinals against Linkopings of Sweden. The Hawks' three second period goals yielded a healthy – but not insurmountable – 3-0 lead at the second intermission. The Lions of the north roared back with four third period goals, and only a desperate rebound score by Vince Hinostroza forced overtime.

After a goalless extra period, neither team converted their first shootout attempt, but both found the net on their second try. Linkopings took a 2-1 shootout lead in the third round, bringing Papa to the ice with the game on his stick.

"If I missed, we would have been playing for bronze the next day. I'd be lying if I said I wasn't nervous when I stepped on the ice for my turn. Somehow the puck found the back of the net and our hopes of moving on continued."

A Hinostroza conversion and McAdam save advanced Waterloo to the gold medal matchup.

Unfortunately, Waterloo's high-scoring offense – responsible for 22 goals in the first five games – gave out the next day. Scoreless against the Sudbury Wolves going to the third period, the Canadians went ahead with just over 12 minutes to play. A power play goal less than a minute later put the game out of reach; the Hawks accepted silver medals after the 2-0 loss.

For McCoshen, McAdam, Papa, and the Hawks' other veterans, it was the second winner-take-all loss in a championship setting in three months. During May, much of the team had suffered a Game Five defeat in the Clark Cup Championship Series against the Green Bay Gamblers.

"Honestly, the loss in Russia was nowhere near as painful to swallow as the defeat in Game Five of the Clark Cup Championship," noted McCoshen. "The emotional investment and physical nature of playing nearly two months of playoff hockey with your best friends simply does not compare to the Russia tournament."

Papa pointed out that the losses did not overshadow the achievements which the Hawks accomplished in both circumstances.

"No one really gave us a shot to beat Canada, I don't think, let alone make the finals; yet, we were tied 0-0 going into the third period. The same can be said against the Gamblers. They perhaps had one the best regular season performances ever with only nine losses. Most people didn't think anyone had a shot to beat them, but we took them to Game Five in a best-of-five series."

McAdam was named the tournament's best goaltender, and recalled, "Having success against great players from other parts of the world really helped going forward by giving me the confidence I needed to compete at a high level."

According to McCoshen, the long trip was worth it, beyond the silver medal.

"Playing in Russia was an advantage for our 2012/13 Black Hawks squad. We started the year really well…I would say it was positive initially for our club…We were playing meaningful games since mid-August, nearly two months before the USHL season even started."

During the 2012/13 campaign which followed, the Hawks tied a then-team record with 39 wins and set a new mark for goals with 273.

"I feel extremely blessed to have had the opportunity to be a part of that trip, and I made many memories that will last me a lifetime," concluded McAdam.

It's not clear how the United States and Russia will see each other in 2022 on the tenth anniversary of Waterloo's Junior Club World Cup silver medal. Regardless of the relationship between the two countries, players from Waterloo and fans from Omsk are likely to still think back on each other with fond memories.

Black Hawks vs. China, 2010

Another article associated with the 2022 Winter Olympics, this recap of an international exhibition appeared on waterlooblackhawks.com February 4, 2022.

The 2022 Beijing Olympics are underway. Even before the grandeur of the official opening ceremonies on Friday, competition has already started. That includes the Women's Olympic Hockey preliminaries, with perennial favorites Team USA and Canada, plus countries as diverse as Denmark, Japan, and the host Chinese.

Winter athletes from all over the world have made their way to the venues where they will compete, and anticipation has been building for the next two weeks of competition.

Nearly a dozen years ago, a group of Chinese hockey players arrived at Young Arena in Waterloo. There was far less fanfare for a single Sunday afternoon of international hockey, but the day provided three memorable periods for the Black Hawks who participated, plus the small group of fans in attendance.

The initial 2010/11 Black Hawks roster included 18-year-old forward Guan Wang. His father, Anfu, had come to the United States after first taking the ice in his native China, rising as far as that country's national team. Eventually as a student at Iowa State University, Anfu joined the school's club team and helped the Cyclones to an ACHA National Championship. A generation later, Guan was hoping for his own college hockey opportunity by way of the USHL.

"He was a great teammate and person as well," remembered Hawks goalie Eamon McAdam, who was simultaneously seeing the USHL for the first time that fall. "[Guan] was always very kind to me, and I can't remember one time where anyone was mad or even frustrated with him. Just a quiet, positive person."

Through Anfu, the Black Hawks were notified about a Chinese team traveling through North America, looking for games that autumn. Would Waterloo be interested in an exhibition just a few weeks after the USHL regular season had started?

"Conversations about the game started around the locker room midweek," said forward Tyler Zepeda, who was playing his second season as a Black Hawk in 2010/11. "The chatter was we were going to be playing a game Sunday. Normally this would be our day off. I think for me personally, my thoughts were it was exciting to be a part of an event that I may never get a chance to do again."

The game was penciled in for October 10th, with puck drop less than 24 hours after a 5-3 Saturday night win against the Lincoln Stars that evened the Hawks' season record at 1-1-0. When the Chinese team arrived around 2 p.m. that day, it quickly became clear that the matchup would be somewhat different than expected. Waterloo officials thought they would be hosting the Chinese National Junior Team, perhaps en route to skating in a lower division of the IIHF World Junior Championships. Instead, the players who stepped off the bus were part of a touring pro squad from Harbin, a city in northern China. As it turned out, they ranged in age from 18 to 37.

"One of my most distinct memories of the game was when we were skating around in warmups and looking across the ice," said McAdam. "We all started to look at each other in shock, because we were so surprised how old everyone seemed. There were guys with five o'clock shadows and mustaches. For me as a 16-year-old, I was getting a bit nervous to play against those guys."

In McAdam's case, that surprise came on top of the tension created by appearing in his very first game for Waterloo. He was the Hawks' third goalie that season, practicing with the team but technically on the affiliate list. Only Ian McCoshen – who had just turned 15 two months earlier – was younger.

For Zepeda, the age difference of the visitors was immaterial compared to having no scouting report.

"We didn't know anything about them…We were unsure of how the game would play out, whether it would be physical or skilled," he said. "Honestly, I had no idea about the age difference until we got done with the game."

Meanwhile, the Black Hawks front office was sent scrambling to address last-minute challenges. What were the formalities for an international game? Was it necessary to present a gift to the visiting coaches or players? Was the Chinese national anthem available to play from YouTube before the opening faceoff? If this wasn't China's National Junior squad, was there a roster available?

When the player list was pieced together, it showed at least six members of the 2010 Chinese MEN'S National Team.

The game had been publicized less than a week earlier. The curious matchup at the rink was not enough to convince most hockey fans to change their plans for a warm mid-October Sunday. A crowd of only several hundred people had found their seats by the time the two national anthems played.

It took a Waterloo power play for the Hawks to record the day's first goal. Jacob MacDonald whistled a wrister into the net from the top of the right circle almost six minutes into the game. The Hawks stacked up three more goals near the end of the period from Jamie Hill, Luke Hannon, and James Hansen. Guan Wang had the lone assist on Hansen's goal.

After a scoreless second, Waterloo added three more in the third period. Tyson Fulton, Alex Guptill, and Hannon were responsible. The Hawks outshot Harbin 47-9 in the 7-0 victory. If McAdam was apprehensive, teammates in front of him made it an easier day than expected. The 16-year-old pitched a shutout the first time he put on a Waterloo jersey in a game situation.

As the season continued, McAdam had the chance to play in four regular season games, winning twice. Zepeda led the 2010/11 Hawks with 31 points (15 goals, 16 assists), despite missing six of 60 regular season games. In a tough year, Waterloo clawed into the last playoff spot during the spring of 2011.

Yet for a number of players, that winter would be foundational to great success in the seasons which followed. Waterloo reached the Clark Cup Championship series against Green Bay at the end of the 2011/12 campaign, with bigger contributions from players like McAdam, McCoshen, and Vinnie Hinostroza, who had all been among the youngest Hawks at the time of the Harbin exhibition. Then in August of 2012, Waterloo's next international experience happened on a truly world stage. Behind McAdam's play as the most valuable goaltender at the Junior Club World Cup, the Hawks won a silver medal representing the United States in Omsk, Russia.

Zepeda was not among the players who spent two summer weeks in Siberia. He had moved on to college in the fall of 2012 following three years with the Hawks.

"I missed the trip to Russia that happened the year after I had left," said Zepeda, still disappointed. "For me – and I would argue that most players would agree – it's an honor to represent and play for your country, no matter what sport or event."

In McAdam's case, his initial junior hockey appearance against Harbin – the first time he had ever seen an opponent from outside North America – perhaps foreshadowed the direction hockey has now taken him. After being drafted by the New York Islanders, playing for Penn State, and minding the crease for several AHL and ECHL teams over five seasons, this winter McAdam is playing in Denmark.

"It was always such a special experience growing up playing against foreign opponents, even teams from Canada," McAdam reflected. "You always thought they were so different from you for any number of reasons. Expectations were always high going into those games.

"It is so funny now, playing professionally over in Europe, and looking back on all those expectations of the kids being so dramatically different. That idea was so off base. Hockey is such a small world and kids all across the world have such similar stories in the locker room about growing up in hockey. You see it now that we're all grown up and playing together."

More than a decade has passed since Waterloo and Harbin represented their countries in a friendly Cedar Valley exhibition in front of a smattering of spectators. Undoubtedly, there will be a few more eyes on Beijing when the United States meets China during the Olympics one week from today.

Lifting Hockey in the Land of the Rising Sun

This article about Yuki Miura appeared in Hawk Tawk Mag-e-Zine *during February 2017, amid his lone winter in Waterloo. After college, Miura returned to Eastern Iowa and established himself as a regular with the Iowa Heartlanders of the ECHL.*

Yuki Miura has enjoyed his season with the Waterloo Black Hawks. He has fond memories of the last two seasons he spent in Czech Republic skating for HC Kladno. No amount of snow or cold can dampen his outlook for the 2017/18 season, in which he will move on to the frigid shorelines of Sault Ste. Marie, Michigan, while attending Lake Superior State University.

But Miura has one grand aspiration for his hockey career.

"My dream is to play in the Olympics," he says, well aware that Japan's Olympic ice hockey history has been fleeting.

Nearly 50 years ago, another Japanese player came to the Cedar Valley with similar thoughts. Yaz Tanaka was dispatched to the United States to learn the finer points of the game ahead of the 1972 Sapporo Olympics. As the host nation, Japan had the opportunity to field a team, although they had limited experience in the sport. Still, they finished ninth in the 11-team event, ahead of Switzerland and Yugoslavia.

Two-and-a-half decades later, Miura was barely walking when his father, Takayuki, took the ice for the Japanese National Team during the 1998 Winter Olympics in Nagano. Again, the country's hockey community had an opportunity to play in front of home fans at the most prestigious of international events. During a preliminary stage, Japan lost twice and tied a third game. The host country ultimately won once during the tournament, a 13th-place game against Austria.

Japan has not returned to the Olympics since.

"I think that's why ice hockey is not a popular sport in Japan. My dream is to lead the team to the Olympics, and I want to make ice hockey popular in Japan."

While other children his age were playing baseball or soccer, Miura began to spend his days at the rink when he was five. He dabbled in speed skating, judo, and even figure skating, all with an eye toward using elements of those sports to improve his hockey skills.

To raise his chances of becoming an elite player, he left Japan to play with the Czechs, whose fathers had won gold in Nagano.

"The people were very kind. In Czech Republic, we used all Olympic-sized rinks, so I had time to make plays. The Czech style is 'pass, pass, pass, then shoot'…I learned that communication is really important. At first, I couldn't speak the Czech language, but I learned a lot and finally I could."

Last season with Kladno, Miura was among the league's best offensive players. He racked up a league-high 33 goals in just 38 games, tallying another 29 assists.

Time in Europe helped Mura earn multiple assignments with his country's national program, including experience at a second tier of the World Junior Championships. Seeking another opportunity to represent Japan in 2016, he connected with former Black Hawk Yuri Terao.

"I met him in a national team tryout camp, and he told me how to play in the U.S.A., and how good Waterloo is, and that's why I am here now," Miura remembers. "It was a really big decision for me, because after last season, my senior team in Czech Republic suggested to me [signing a] professional contract, but I wanted to play in the NCAA and the USHL."

Entering February, Miura's season with the Hawks has included appearances in all but four games. He has seen some power play time, accumulating four of his 11 points in special teams situations. Miura's best performance came in Waterloo's highest-scoring game. Visiting the Sioux Falls Stampede on October 15th, he was the only Hawk to record multiple goals during a 9-5 win.

Miura admits that his circumstances produce pressure to perform at that level with more consistency. He came to Waterloo at age 20 and as an international import, two categories for which league rosters are tightly limited.

"I have really good teammates and good staff and good friends," Miura says. "I don't have many points now. We have only 22 games left, then playoffs. The first half of the season, I didn't play well, so the last 22 games and the playoffs, I really want to help the team."

During the more-than-four months since the season began, Miura has developed a sincere admiration for his teammates, as much for their approach to life away from the game as for what they do on the ice.

"I was very surprised that most of the guys were younger than me," he says of his arrival. "They all have a vision of the people they want to be. In Japan, the young guys don't have a plan…That's why the U.S.A. is really good…I learned that young Japanese guys have to think more and more about what they want to be."

For Miura, that suggests a long-term future in the business of sports to one day help develop another generation of enthusiastic Japanese athletes for the game.

"If we want to be a better hockey country, we have to play overseas. I played in Czech Republic and now I'm playing in the U.S., and I want to use that experience for the young kids of the future."

After skating for Lake Superior State, Miura – like the rest of his Waterloo teammates – would like the opportunity to play professional hockey in North America. At some point, he would also like to return to Czech Republic at a senior level.

"When I was there, a lot of people helped me. It was a really good place with good people, so someday I want to go back to Czech Republic and play for everyone who helped me."

And of course, Miura contemplates what might be possible in his country if his generation can bring Japan back to the Olympics or raise the nation's profile in the International Ice Hockey Federation World Championships.

However, at this moment, Miura also sees a special opportunity while he is in northeast Iowa.

"We have a chance to get the Clark Cup. I am very proud to be a Hawk, and I want to help the team."

Cassetti Takes Giant Step

On Christmas Day, 2024, this story was posted as part of the "Where Are They Now" series on waterlooblackhawks.com.

Boston University traveled over 2,900 miles to win a holiday hockey tournament last month.

The opponents were familiar: the Terriers' initial victory during the Friendship Four was against conference rival Merrimack. BU followed up the next night by beating former Hockey East foe Notre Dame. A three-goal third period gave Boston University a 4-3 decision and the Belpot Trophy.

The team's terrier mascot was on the ice for a celebratory photo. School pep bands had been playing throughout the two days of competition. The student sections were boisterous, and Boston University jerseys were readily seen, as well as those worn by Merrimack, Notre Dame, and Harvard fans.

Only the setting was out of the ordinary: SSE Arena is a short walk from the *Titanic* museum, beside the River Lagan, just upstream from the Belfast Lough. The rink is more regularly home to the Belfast Giants, Northern Ireland's team in the Elite Ice Hockey League. It's also the rink where former Waterloo Black Hawk forward Joe Cassetti is spending his first season in pro hockey.

Just a year removed from skating in the NCAA, Cassetti saw many familiar faces as relatives of former teammates and opponents made their way to SSE Arena for the Friendship Four.

"They were just talking about how much they loved it here," says Cassetti, reflecting on the Thanksgiving week visitors. "It's cool when you walk downtown…there's a bunch of pubs and just cool places to eat, and everything seems really kind of cozy and warm."

Cassetti has spent most of his life as a hockey nomad. Originally from California, he was playing AAA hockey in Michigan during his early teens. That led to a two-year stint with the National Team Development Program and three seasons in Waterloo (mixing in a semester at Merrimack). Cassetti settled in at Miami University from 2020 to 2023 before moving on to Western Michigan last year for his final season of college hockey, skating as a member of the Broncos and going to class as a graduate student in Kalamazoo.

When the college season ended last spring, Cassetti admits he wasn't sure what would be next. However, his agent and Giants executives were already well-acquainted, opening up his opportunity in the EIHL.

"It seemed like a great fit for me and something I definitely wanted to experience, coming out to Northern Ireland. And here I am," says Cassetti.

Like many North American players, the 25-year-old forward is taking advantage of tuition and educational support which is commonly offered by EIHL clubs. It's one of the features which tends to attract players across the Atlantic. In Cassetti's case, he is attending online classes offered by Lasell University in Boston. He expects to earn his Master of Business Administration this spring.

On the ice, the Olympic-sized dimensions in EIHL buildings are familiar. Cassetti enjoyed success on Young Arena's wide rink, and before that, he had seen the wider surfaces during international competition with the NTDP.

Perhaps the biggest adjustment is being a rookie again.

"I went from being one of the oldest guys in college last year – especially on my team – to now I'm the youngest [here]," Cassetti says. "Some of my teammates are married or have kids, and that's a little different, playing older guys, but that's super fun too. You get to learn a lot of stuff, hear some funny stories. A lot of them come from college hockey in America too, so it's all very relatable."

The big forward had a good start. He notched a pair of goals during his debut against the Dundee Stars on September 7th. The Giants won 7-3. In fact, Belfast opened with four wins, and Cassetti stacked up four points (three goals, one assist). However, his rookie season took an unfortunate turn even before it was a month old. Cassetti dislocated his shoulder, leading to surgery in late October.

"I'm just working on my shoulder, on the mend, not really sure what my timeline is…aiming towards the end of the season," Cassetti explains. "[I'll] hopefully be able to get back in the lineup and help the team out, but it's still month-by-month right now, week-by-week. Just seeing how it feels."

The injury has provided an unexpected quantity of additional time to experience Northern Ireland. Cassetti concedes he is still adjusting to Irish accents and driving on the left side of the road. However it was no challenge to embrace the traditional Sunday roast, a savory weekly dinner of beef, potatoes, and vegetables.

Being sidelined for most of the season has also meant the chance to reconnect with some old friends under less adversarial conditions than if those reunions had been on the ice.

"A couple months ago, Coventry came here – the Coventry Blaze – and they stayed the night. I was able to go see two of my former teammates from Miami and one of my former teammates from Merrimack, who's actually the assistant coach [for Coventry] now.

"Hockey's such a small world. Guys I was playing against in juniors – when I was playing in Waterloo – I ended up playing with them in college, and so forth and so on. It's kind of a full-circle moment, seeing some of these guys on the other side, but it's really cool that we're all across the Atlantic and still keeping up with our friendships and communicating."

Cassetti's family has also been to Belfast to see his new surroundings.

"My grandma on my dad's side was 100 percent Irish. Her family came from the southern region, near Cork, I believe," say Cassetti. "My dad just got to come out with my little brother. That was really cool, [because Ireland] was the one country that my dad's always wanted to go to and take his dad to. Unfortunately, he [Cassetti's grandfather] is not with us anymore, but you know, he would have been really happy about this whole opportunity."

As for younger players like the ones who were in Belfast last month for the Friendship Four, Cassetti is more than willing to recommend the professional playing experience in Europe.

"I haven't really been to too many other European countries, but everyone I know that's made the transition from North American hockey – whether it's the ECHL, the AHL, the NHL – and ended up coming over here: a lot of guys say that they wish they would have experienced Europe sooner.

"It's a really cool experience, and there's not many other jobs away from hockey that would ever take me to Belfast, or anywhere else in Europe for that matter. It's just a really cool, once-in-a-lifetime opportunity and something that is so special about hockey."

Clearly four months in Ireland has made a lasting impression on the former Black Hawk. Cassetti will have his chance to make an impression on Belfast hockey fans when he is back on the ice in 2025.

Excused Absences from Orientation Camp

Brown, Erdman Away at Hlinka Gretzky Cup

Griffin Erdman and Connor Brown shared their thoughts about an August trip to the Hlinka Gretzky Cup competition as the cover story for the October 2022 Hawk Tawk Mag-e-Zine.

Prospective Black Hawks players had a lot to play for during the closing days of July. For many of the skaters who were at Young Arena, their place on this year's team was not yet secure. A few were already hoping to make an impression for the 2023/24 season. Yet with whatever tension there may have been in Waterloo at that time, there were no medals for the winners, no stats, and certainly no national TV coverage.

Forwards Connor Brown and Griffin Erdman were elsewhere. The games they were playing included all of those peripheral considerations, plus the chance to skate for the United States of America.

The annual Hlinka Gretzky Cup tournament is a summer tradition, hosted either in Czechia and Slovakia, or in Canada. The 2022 event was held in Red Deer, Alberta. Besides teams of Americans, Canadians, Czechs, and Slovaks, players from Finland, Sweden, Switzerland, and Germany represented their countries. All of the participants this year were born in 2005, and most will be eligible for the NHL Draft in 2023.

The Hlinka Gretzky Cup has been a significant – if brief – stop for many Black Hawks on their way to the NHL. Since 2011, Cal Petersen, Vinnie Hinostroza, Brock Boeser, Tom Novak, Mikey Anderson, and Jack Drury have all represented the U.S., with each of those stars later drafted after finding success during a full season in Waterloo.

To get to Red Deer this summer, the process began in Buffalo a month earlier, with a camp for prospective players hoping to make the U.S. Under-18 Men's Select roster.

"I think there were around 200 players there, and they broke us up into teams to play games for a week," says Erdman. "At the end, they picked an All-Star camp, and during the weekend, we played two games from this 40-man group."

Erdman concedes being nervous until his name was announced as part of the final roster. For Brown, a successful rookie season in the USHL gave him a high level of confidence, but he acknowledges that the camp and the tournament featured the best players among his peers.

"It was awesome getting to know all the guys that are so talented and getting to play with them. It's obviously the best of the best there for our age group, so it's definitely a hard tournament, and that's what was most fun about it."

Weeks before the Buffalo camp, Brown and Erdman had skated during the Hawks' first summer ice, lessening the impact of being absent for the late July session in Waterloo.

"It was definitely not a good thing missing it," Brown says, "But I stayed in the loop with all the guys here, and we talked about our season and what we're looking forward to."

For the Hawks, having Brown and Erdman training and playing at a high level all summer will hopefully be more valuable in the long run than anything they could have done at Young Arena. The extra time they spent as teammates could mean fast dividends.

"Me and Brownie actually got a chance to play together on the line, and that was super fun," Erdman says, adding, "We had a great connection and scored some big goals."

The results in Red Deer were not up to expectations for Erdman, Brown, and their teammates. After an 8-1 opening game win versus Germany, the U.S. team was held to one goal by Finland, then similarly limited in a loss to Czechia, before edging Slovakia 4-2 in their tournament finale to take fifth place. Erdman finished with a goal and two assists.

"I think we underperformed to say the least," Erdman noted. "With the talent we had, we probably could have been in the gold medal game. We got into some penalty trouble against Finland and the Czechs."

"Discipline was a big part of it for us," agreed Brown. "I thought if we had more discipline, we would have gone a lot farther."

Besides playing together, Brown and Erdman had the opportunity to become familiar with several other USHL personalities. The U.S. team was led by Tri-City Head Coach Anthony Noreen, with Des Moines' Matt Curley serving as an assistant. Already during the earliest days of this USHL season, recent teammates like Andrew Strathmann and Will Whitelaw – each in their first seasons with the Youngstown Phantoms – have become opponents.

"Seeing them, competing against them [during the Fall Classic], it's always fun," says Erdman. "They're great players, so it's always a good battle."

Brown summed up his lasting impressions from Red Deer, saying, "It was awesome getting to be on NHL Network where all your family and friends from back home can see you. It was also great to bond with our teammates there in all the special ways we got to know each other playing for our country."

For Brown and Erdman – with the draft nine months away – the Hlinka Gretzky Cup may not be the last time they're on NHL Network.

Beginning in the Middle, Preparing for the End

A strong Black Hawks team became even better after midseason trades detailed in this March 2017 article for Hawk Tawk Mag-e-Zine.

In the late months of hockey season one year ago, Alex Limoges saw a good team become a champion.

The Tri-City Storm stayed at or near the top of the Western Conference throughout 2015/16. Despite having fewer wins than any other team which qualified for the Clark Cup Playoffs, points from overtime games helped Tri-City climb to the regular season conference championship. They went on to win the Clark Cup, too.

"I'm going to remember the guys in the locker room," Limoges says. "The mentality and the energy there…we knew we could do it, but it wasn't overconfidence. It was just an unbelievable experience for me."

Max Humitz and Brandon Duhaime had only been Limoges' teammates for a matter of weeks before the Clark Cup Playoffs began. Both proved to be valuable acquisitions as the Storm played to the end of May.

In Game Three of a first round series against the Sioux Falls Stampede, Humitz scored early in the second period, spurring a rally which turned a 1-0 deficit into a 4-1 series-clinching road victory. He also scored twice during the next round against the Black Hawks, including the first goal in what eventually became a 5-3 Game Five win, advancing the Storm to the Clark Cup Championship series.

Duhaime had the go-ahead goal which put Tri-City ahead for good in Game Five versus the Hawks. He also set the final score in Game Three of the Finals against the Dubuque Fighting Saints, recording an empty-netter, which all but started the Storm's championship celebration in front of a euphoric home crowd.

A year after Humitz and Duhaime arrived in Kearney, Limoges finds himself in a similar position coming to Waterloo. He has joined a Black Hawks squad dreaming of a spectacular finish to a good season. Limoges is in Waterloo because he is a player who can help make it happen.

"The team is hot right now. It's fun to join a winning team," he says, adding, "Tri-City was great to me, and I owe a lot to those guys, but I'm excited to get the new start and make a run for the Cup."

The former Tri-City captain has taken on an important assignment in Waterloo: skating as the third member of Waterloo's highly skilled line which includes scoring stars Nick Swaney and Shane Bowers.

"We all complement each other's game. We can move the puck quickly, we know the right spots, and each one of us can score…it's been working out well so far."

Limoges is one of a handful of players added since Christmas as the Hawks have evolved in 2016/17. Goaltender Peter Thome arrived around the same time. Fellow forward Sam Craggs came to Waterloo in late January. Defensemen Ethan Spaxman and Grant Gabriele were added to the roster just after the holiday break; they had the first chance to make an impact.

Both Spaxman and Gabriele added size and veteran poise. For Gabriele, this is the second straight year he has joined a playoff contender midway through the season, but in 2015/16, circumstances didn't work out during his time with the Muskegon Lumberjacks.

"When I got there, we were doing well, and toward the end of the season, we didn't have the best final stretch…just kind of an unfortunate ending," Gabriele remembers.

The defenseman calls last season a learning experience, adding that he doesn't feel any extra pressure as a late addition to a strong Hawks roster.

"I'm just here trying to play and have fun. When I came here, I thought whatever I could do to help the team win and make the playoffs, that's what I'm going to do."

The Hawks are Gabriele's fifth United States Hockey League club after appearances with the National Team Development Program, Omaha Lancers, Chicago Steel, and Muskegon. That gives his praise for what he found in Waterloo extra weight.

"I was really impressed, especially the first game here at home, I was just blown away at the atmosphere; the fans here are just die-hard Black Hawks fans," he says, continuing, "It's like a pro atmosphere. You've got guys like "T" and "Spens" [trainer Todd Klein and strength coach Spenser Popinga] just constantly doing stuff for us…a great coaching staff…just the overall feel is an NHL experience."

Like Limoges, Gabriele has stepped into a prominent role for Waterloo. The recently minted Ohio State recruit is an important point man on the Black Hawks' power play. Through the end of February, Gabriele has three goals – all on special teams – plus six assists in 21 appearances.

Playing time for Limoges and Gabriele was never in question. For a goalie, the transition to a new team can sometimes be more tenuous.

Thome explains, "You just have to make sure you're ready to do your job and be a good teammate and not come in with a big ego. Just be a good teammate and show up every day and do the right things to try and get better.

"There's only one net, so you've got to go in and earn every minute you get in the blue paint. It is different, but I've been fortunate that PK trusted me right away and let me step in my second game as part of the Black Hawks."

That strong initial showing has opened more opportunities for Thome, especially as the Hawks rest Robbie Beydoun after a minor lower body injury suffered in mid-February.

"The guys had been great right away at making me feel welcome," Thome says. "Obviously you become closer with the guys as you battle with them on Friday and Saturday nights. You play those games and you get confidence just being around the guys; you're part of the team and not just on the sidelines watching."

Thome spent last season in the North American Hockey League. His performance for the Aberdeen Wings was good enough to make him one of the NAHL's elite goalies, and he was drafted by the NHL's Columbus Blue Jackets last summer.

However, the Wings missed the Robertson Cup playoffs.

"You play the 60 games to get to the playoffs, and you play the playoffs for a chance to win a championship. I'm excited just at the possibility of making the playoffs and making a run…just doing what I can to be ready when the puck drops."

Since the start of February, good results have followed Waterloo whenever and wherever the puck has been in play. Limoges – who averaged more than a point per game in February – sums up his experience during one month as a Black Hawk.

"I haven't been here for too long, but it's a great team atmosphere, and everybody seems to be pulling the right way."

And, pulling the right direction is a little easier when experienced hands join in to tow Waterloo toward playoff hockey.

JT Brown Proving Hockey is His Game

Minnesota-based publication Let's Play Hockey *requested this update on Minnesota native JT Brown for their February 5, 2009 edition.*

There wasn't any question JT Brown was going to wear shoulder pads and a helmet. What did need to be decided was whether the son of former Minnesota Vikings running back Ted Brown would have football cleats or hockey skates.

"I really decided that hockey was what I wanted in the ninth and tenth grades," says the younger Brown. "I played football and baseball, but I kind of toned those down, because I didn't want to get hurt for hockey."

Brown's 5-foot, 10-inch, 165-pound frame may have also made him better suited for a spot on right wing than in the backfield. His skills on the ice confirmed the decision. Averaging more than two points-per-game as a senior at Rosemount High School last year, Brown was a finalist for the coveted Mr. Hockey award.

Waterloo Black Hawks assistant coach Shane Fukushima scouted Brown and was impressed with his puck-handling skills.

"At the high school level, JT always had the puck on his stick," recalls Fukushima. "He had the ability to control the entire game by himself."

The Black Hawks selected Brown in the sixth round of the United States Hockey League Entry Draft last May. As a rookie coming to junior hockey, Brown was forced to prove himself and step up his game.

"Going from high school to the camps, it was faster. Even from camps just to the preseason, and then from preseason to the regular season games, the pace of play is really a lot faster than high school," says Brown.

Adding a degree of difficulty to the transition was a wrist injury the 19-year-old suffered in one of Waterloo's first preseason games. His debut as a Black Hawk was delayed two months as he recovered and watched from the stands. When he did hit the ice, it didn't take Brown long to find his stride; he had five points in his first five USHL games. By last weekend, his speed and playmaking ability had him skating with Waterloo's starting line, alongside the league's second-leading scorer Craig Smith and Bowling Green-bound Jordan Samuels-Thomas.

Brown has also had a chance to wear the same sweater as one of his former rivals, Tyler Barnes, who was also a Mr. Hockey finalist playing for Burnsville last winter.

"I didn't like playing against Barnes," Brown admits, "because he was good and he'd always score on us, so now he's on this team and that just helps us out.

"I like playing against some of the guys that were on my high school team, [now] playing for other USHL teams. You feel like you know what their strengths are, and you know how to beat them."

Brown didn't commit to post-USHL plans while in high school, but Fukushima expects him to literally grow into a significant college prospect.

"He has to gain more strength and weight before he can be effective on a consistent basis, in this league and beyond. I think that will come with maturity and attention to detail, on and off the ice," says Fukushima.

While Waterloo, Iowa, isn't too far from home, Brown is keeping his options open for college.

"It would be nice to be close to home," Brown says, "but that's not shutting down any options. I wouldn't mind playing hockey anywhere…If that's in Minnesota or somewhere near here, that's good, but if it's away from home…that's still good."

[Postscript – Brown played college hockey for Minnesota-Duluth, then reached the NHL with the Tampa Bay Lightning.]

Black Hawks Head Coach Earns 300th Victory

PK O'Handley achieved many additional milestones after this article appeared in The Iowa Sports Connection *Volume 9, Issue 8 – November 2007. O'Handley went on to a career total of 778 wins (638 of them with the Black Hawks). He was the first coach on the bench for 1,000 regular season USHL games. In 2013/14, he overtook Mike Hastings for the most wins in league history.*

Superior, Wisconsin is a hard-working, industrial town sitting just across the state line from its twin port, Duluth. The weather and demographics are conducive to ice hockey. Collars are just as blue in Waterloo, Iowa, where John Deere and other manufacturers employ many, and hockey has its own tradition and popularity. The game has led PK O'Handley from one location to the other.

The head coach of the Waterloo Black Hawks earned his 300th United States Hockey League win early this season. All 300 victories have come while leading teams from Iowa. O'Handley spent seven seasons in Mason City with the North Iowa Huskies and, after a foray into professional hockey, is in his sixth year with the Black Hawks.

The USHL is the nation's top junior hockey league. Players hope to move into the NCAA and some go from there to the professional ranks. Iowa is home to five of the league's twelve teams: the Black Hawks, Des Moines Buccaneers, Cedar Rapids Rough Riders, Sioux City Musketeers, and Omaha Lancers (who play in Council Bluffs). Still, hockey doesn't immediately come to mind when most people think of the Hawkeye State.

"First of all, I didn't know I was going to become a hockey coach," O'Handley says. "I thought I was still going to be a player at this time, or in business, or doing something. To say I would have done it in the state of Iowa, I would have told you you were crazy, but things have a funny way of working out, and it couldn't have worked out better."

O'Handley had to work for his first USHL win with North Iowa in 1991. His Huskies lost the season-opener in Des Moines 13-2, then fell at home against Thunder Bay 10-1.

"And that was after winning the Buc Bowl [preseason tournament] and everyone telling us how great we were going to be," he remembers.

The first of now-more-than 300 wins eventually came against Dubuque in the season's third game. By 1995/96, O'Handley was able to help the Huskies to just their second season over .500 in franchise history. Two years later, North Iowa won its division.

"For me, there's a little satisfaction that we went from not very good to a pretty good hockey team and left a mark." O'Handley points out that Mason City still has a junior team, the North Iowa Outlaws of the NAHL, that is thriving.

Estero, Florida was O'Handley's next stop. Former Des Moines Head Coach Bob Ferguson, the USHL's winningest coach, was given charge of the expansion Florida Everblades of the professional East Coast Hockey League. O'Handley was Ferguson's assistant and also worked with other affiliates of the Carolina Hurricanes.

In 2002 however, he returned to the USHL with Waterloo to be closer to his family. Since 1979/80, the USHL's first season after transitioning from a semi-professional circuit, the Black Hawks had only finished with more wins than losses in three seasons.

"The attitude around the team was not good…'You know, whatever,' let anything go…I think by changing the culture, my beliefs were you'd have success," he says.

The year O'Handley took over, the Hawks went 38-17-5, just one win shy of taking the USHL's regular season championship, the Anderson Cup. The next season, 2003/04, Waterloo won the Clark Cup title as the USHL's playoff champs. Last year, the Hawks set a new franchise record for wins with 39, captured the elusive Anderson Cup, and finished runners-up for the Clark Cup. After winning both of the league's titles, O'Handley says there are other parts of the job that are even more rewarding.

"It's about the people, the kids, and giving them opportunities to move on, and maybe teaching them a little bit about life and a little bit about hockey. I just want them to say 'It was an experience and I learned'."

Also learning are O'Handley assistants, Shane Fukushima and Derrick Johnson, both from Northwest Wisconsin like O'Handley and both former players from North Iowa.

"Shane is an "X" and "O," very good hockey coach," O'Handley says, "Very good recruiter, very good identifier of talent. There's always a job in hockey for someone like that.

"The chance for Derrick to go to the National Hockey League is great based on his knowledge of computers and video breakdown…putting it into a form that players understand."

Before the players or assistants make it big, however O'Handley hopes their experience with the Hawk changes how they approach the game and life.

"I'm a firm believer in attitude. You look at the successful teams and you have a collective group that bought in and goes to work."

Just like the people in Superior and Waterloo.

Petersen Makes USHL Debut

This article was written in the weeks after Waterloo native Cal Petersen played in his first USHL game during the 2011/12 season.

It's a long ride from Waterloo to Sioux City, and in the winter, there's not much to look at. For 17-year-old Cal Petersen however, the bus trip he made down Highway 20 in late December must have been one of the most exciting of his life.

The goaltender was about to become the first Waterloo native in more than a decade to appear in a regular season game for his hometown Black Hawks, members of the junior-level United States Hockey League. While the Hawks and the USHL were close in proximity for Petersen as he grew up, the top echelon of the sport for players his age was not easy to get to just because the rink was only a few miles away.

Petersen watched from the Black Hawks' bench as an emergency-only backup goalie during several games in the 2009/10 season. The same year, he led the Waterloo Warriors high school team to a junior varsity championship in the Midwest High School Hockey League. Petersen left Waterloo in the fall of 2010 with the hope of returning as a Black Hawk. He joined the Chicago Young Americans, a Tier I midget hockey program.

"It's probably a different route than a lot of people have," says Petersen. "I'm just fortunate that there's an organization that I'm a part of that's in my hometown, and if one of the sacrifices to be on that team is to go to another city and play and progress, then that's a sacrifice that I'm more than willing to make every time."

The Young Americans are coached by Gregg Naumenko, a former professional goalie for the Anaheim Ducks and a protégé of Black Hawks Head Coach PK O'Handley while both were with the North Iowa Huskies in the late 1990's. Petersen excelled during his first midget season, winning 13 of 24 games – including four shutouts – and stopping 92.3 percent of the shots he faced. Watching his progress closely, the Hawks drafted him during the 13th round of the USHL Entry Draft the following summer. More good news came in July when Petersen was selected to join the U.S. Under-18 Select team for the Ivan Hlinka Memorial Tournament in Slovakia.

Back stateside for the USHL preseason in September, Petersen was not able to unseat a pair of veteran goalies already on the Black Hawks roster and returned to the Young Americans with the promise that he would have a shot in the USHL at some point during 2011/12.

"It has been a little bit of a struggle just to stay patient," admitted the 6-foot, 2-inch, 180-pound netminder, "but I have very strong faith in the coaching staff here and also for my midget team at CYA, and I believe that they have my best in [mind with] whatever they're going to do with me, and...whatever they say, I feel it goes, so it's all on their timeline."

His opportunity arrived with a small window in the midget hockey schedule just after Christmas, coinciding with the Hawks' trip to visit the Sioux City Musketeers. Petersen had been on the ice at the Tyson Event Center just a few months earlier during the preseason USHL Fall Classic.

"There were a lot more scouts at the Fall Classic than there were at that game," remarked Petersen, "So in those regards, it was easier. [I was] used to the locker rooms, used to the setup, and really it was feeling pretty natural."

The Hawks struck first with a goal by Toronto Maple Leafs draft pick Tony Cameranesi 3:48 into the game, but David Goodwin stuffed a rebound chance past Petersen's left pad late in the first period to tie the game at intermission. The lone goal of the second pushed the Hawks back in front again as Petersen's former CYA teammate Ryan Papa scored from a sharp angle when a puck bounced to him off the end glass. The Hawks' Mark Naclerio added to the lead in the third before Brad Robbins fired a shot in over Petersen's glove during a power play with six minutes remaining. Nothing else would get by, however, and an empty net goal in the final minute sealed the victory for the young goalie, who finished the night with 34 saves.

After the game, O'Handley foreshadowed more opportunities for his local rookie.

"Cal earned the right, and I think the guys rallied around him. I think when they saw Cal the Monday night after the [Christmas] break at practice, it was a pretty exciting locker room," said O'Handley, himself a former goalie. "[He] certainly in his first start proved he deserved another one real soon."

Lellig Lands in New Surroundings

Defenseman Hunter Lellig shared observations about his final season of college hockey for this waterlooblackhawks.com story which was first posted on January 5, 2023.

Hunter Lellig is doing what he has always done: taking a regular shift, blocking a lot of shots (he leads his team with 45 blocks in 20 games…that's 50 percent more than the next-highest total), and holding down the fort as a steady defensive defenseman.

The only thing is, he's doing it some place brand new during the winter of 2022/23.

Lellig spent four seasons at Minnesota-Duluth. The Bulldogs' results in that time? A national championship in 2019, COVID washed out the 2020 NCAA Tournament, a Frozen Four appearance in 2021, and then an NCAA regional final last spring.

Now the soon-to-be-24-year-old is midway through his fifth college season, his first at Bowling Green.

"At first I was unsure leaving Duluth," Lellig says. "I had to figure out a place to go and what was going to be the right fit for me for school. Bowling Green was a great fit."

Although Lellig is a Waterloo native, he had already relocated to pursue his hockey aspirations long before joining the Black Hawks. A decade ago, Lellig was skating for the Chicago Mission. His family had relocated, giving him the opportunity to take the ice with – and against – the best players in his age group during his early teens. It was a sacrifice which paid off, landing Lellig in the North American Hockey League for 2016/17 before his eventual Waterloo homecoming the next winter.

That 2017/18 Black Hawks team won the Anderson Cup. Players like Jackson Cates, Jack Drury, and Ben Finkelstein were the stars, with Cates and Finkelstein winning league honors for being the top players at their positions. Drury and goaltender Jared Moe were chosen in the 2018 NHL Draft. Lellig was as quietly effective as ever: 53 games, +12, a relatively high-scoring 11 points (including two game-winning goals), and numerous intangible contributions to team success.

Now he has brought those attributes to a new program. Lellig says relocating to Bowling Green is not quite like being a freshman all over again.

"You're in a bigger role as an older guy and helping younger guys is a huge thing. Being a voice in the locker room is also a big thing, and I think after playing four years of college [hockey]...guys understand that you've been around, you've played on a pretty good team, and you can help this team win."

Although the transfer portal has become a ubiquitous part of any discussion about college sports, Lellig's experience demonstrates that the process is a little different than what many people might imagine. He did have some connections to Bowling Green through former Hawks teammate Evan Dougherty and his Chicago Mission coach Gino Cavallini, but that wasn't what led him there. Nor did he go surf the web looking for hockey programs short on blue line experience.

Lellig started by talking to the UMD coaching staff. Athletics officials filled out the paperwork. Then he waited for his phone to ring and the recruiting process to begin anew.

"You want to go somewhere that they want you, and they think you can help build their team," he says. "They're the only people that know that."

Bowling Green was certainly a good fit for Lellig, the student. He had already wrapped up his undergraduate Finance degree in Duluth. After taking six classes last semester, Lellig is now already halfway to adding an MBA to his resume.

"Classes are a little more in-depth, but for the master's program, we have a cohort of about 25 guys. Four other hockey players are in it too, so it's nice to be with them. You can talk about things, go over things together, and the teachers are super helpful with our situation as athletes."

Lellig's job prospects may still include an entry-level position with shoulder pads and skates, just as much as a wardrobe with sport coats and wingtips. Following his season in Waterloo, Lellig had earned a place in the NHL Central Scouting final rankings. Standing at 6-feet, 2-inches and with a history of winning, even if the NHL doesn't call, it seems likely that some pro team will find his number.

"I haven't really thought about it too much or had conversations with people about it," Lellig says. "I'm trying to focus on where the season's at and where we're trying to get as a team. I think I will have an opportunity to play [pro hockey]; at what level, I'm not sure. We'll cross that bridge when we come to it."

For now, the Falcons are 10-12-0 and .500 in the CCHA. Lellig is certain that Bowling Green can improve on their record and climb in the conference standings during the latter part of the season. After a hockey career filled with successes and repeated instances where his risks have been rewarded, there should be no surprise about his optimism. Things have worked out pretty well so far.

"Going into the portal and leaving a great spot like Duluth, it was scary. I didn't know what it was going to be like, but I'm glad I took the chance. This group of guys is great. The MBA program's great. The other students that I'm with: great. I'm really glad I took the chance, and everything is just more than I could have hoped for."

Relocating to western Ohio seems to have worked out pretty well for this stay-at-home defenseman.

[Postscript – After finishing his college career, Lellig spent the 2023/24 season in professional hockey with the ECHL's Iowa Heartlanders.]

Back from School

Making the Most of a Second Season In the USHL

In February of 2019, veteran forward Emil Ohrvall was the subject of this feature in Hawk Tawk Mag-e-Zine.

Although they have spent most of their lives in Sweden, brothers Jesper and Emil Ohrvall have probably seen more of the United States than most Americans.

Elder brother Jesper arrived first and went to Alaska to join the Fairbanks Ice Dogs of the North American Hockey League in 2014. A year later, and continuing through last spring, he was in upstate New York at Rensselaer Polytechnic Institute. This winter, Jesper is in the Deep South with the Chargers of Alabama-Huntsville to wrap up his NCAA career.

Emil came to North America in 2015.

"It started when my brother came over to play junior hockey," said the younger Ohrvall. "My first time coming over to the U.S. was when I went over to Shattuck[-St. Mary's]. I'd never even been on vacation or any tournaments over here, so it was all new for me."

A season of prep school hockey at the powerhouse program in Faribault, Minnesota, was enough to convince the Waterloo Black Hawks to draft Ohrvall. He delivered a goal in his first game and went on to finish seventh on the 2016/17 team with 32 points (13 goals, 19 assists). Last year, the Ohrvall brothers played on the same ice in Troy, New York.

However, like Jesper, Emil did not stick around to spend this winter with the Engineers. Returning to Waterloo for a final season of junior hockey, Emil Ohrvall became part of a growing trend of players stepping into the Black Hawks' lineup with a season or more of college hockey to his credit.

"It was a good experience. It turned out to be a little different than I had planned when I went in," Ohrvall conceded. "I learned a lot, both as a player and as a person…I think the year in college really helped me, and I've been able to take my game to the next level."

The numbers seem to confirm that Ohrvall is a different player than the one who went to college after the 2016/17 campaign. A force so far this season, the now-20-year-old has far surpassed his scoring figures from two years ago. He already has 21 goals and 22 assists in just 39 games. He leads the Hawks with nine power play goals. Perhaps most impressively, Ohrvall's three hat tricks this season are the most by a Waterloo player since Brock Boeser in 2014/15.

Whatever position Ohrvall occupies on the stat sheet when the current season comes to an end, and however many big games he has when the lights are bright and the stands are full, Black Hawks Head Coach PK O'Handley has seen other changes in the Swedish forward.

"He's actually a better student this time around from the hockey side than he was…which I think happens with age," O'Handley explained, continuing, "Maturity gives you a little more perspective on how to come back, and he's more of a sponge on some of the finer points of what he's aspiring to be."

"All the staff and all the people around here know a lot about hockey, and it's my last chance to soak it up and take in all the information," Ohrvall expounded. "Being a little bit older, I've been growing up a little bit. I just want to learn and educate my game and get better."

Whether it is a chance for more ice time or a second opportunity to find the right school, an increasing number of players have been taking advantage of a season in the USHL after their freshman – or even sophomore – seasons. None have achieved the type of spectacular success Ben Finkelstein found in 2017/18. Between St. Lawrence and Boston College, the Florida Panthers prospect was a Black Hawk for just a few months, but it was enough to earn the USHL's Defenseman of the Year award as Finkelstein churned out an astounding 34 points in 23 games manning the blue line. His arrival was just the boost Waterloo needed to rally for the Anderson Cup last spring.

Even with Finkelstein's success as an example of what is possible, Ohrvall's decision to leave RPI did not come without some risk. As a 20-year-old, Ohrvall cannot play in the USHL after this season, and his plans to attend a new school in the fall have not been finalized. Nevertheless, he is glad to be back in Waterloo colors.

"I was 'all in' on the decision. I knew that coming back to Waterloo, I had the opportunity to do something good."

"I give Emil a lot of credit," adds O'Handley. "I don't think he made the decision lightly. He was pretty calculated with what he was doing, and he'll have a new commitment here relatively shortly."

Before this fall, Ohrvall's last USHL game had been a winner-take-all Game Five matchup versus the Sioux City Musketeers during the 2017 Western Conference Final. The Hawks lost that night at Tyson Events Center. Ohrvall left the rink with Shane Bowers, Nick Swaney, Mikey

Anderson, and several others who believed it was their last game at the junior level. Back in Waterloo this year, Ohrvall found a mostly new group of teammates in the locker room.

"Everything kind of looks the same around here, but it's, for sure, a lot of new faces on the team. It's different; that's junior hockey: teams always look different every year," reflects Ohrvall.

O'Handley says that even players who have spent a season with the Black Hawks need the opportunity to reestablish themselves: "We don't assume that they just come back in and remember everything. Some of the culture things they certainly don't forget, and we tell them that we expect them to be a driving force for [establishing team culture] in the dressing room. On the other side of that, we treat them like every other player; year-to-year, it's back to Hockey 101."

For O'Handley, working with Ohrvall a second time has been gratifying.

"I think he's really confident. He's confident in his shot, he's confident on getting to spots that give him opportunities…he knows where to go on the ice to get himself into a scoring situation."

Knowing where to go might be just what you would expect from a skater who found his way from Sweden to North America and made a mark in prep, junior, and college hockey all within a few short years.

The Declaration – and Determination – of Independents

Black Hawks players were well-represented on the quickly-expanding list of independent NCAA Division I college hockey programs, as noted in this February 8, 2023 article for waterlooblackhawks.com.

Long Island University picked up a pair of wins last weekend. That gives the Sharks five straight victories, the longest winning streak in the program's history. The recent 9-3 and 9-1 results came against Stonehill, and the run started late last month against another fellow NCAA Division I Independent, Lindenwood. In between, the Sharks defeated Princeton 6-4.

The Tigers' hockey heritage – so deep it includes the legendary Hobey Baker – was no help on January 28th.

Freshman and former Black Hawk Tyler Kostelecky was on the ice for the Princeton game. It's one of three NCAA appearances he has made so far. Kostelecky's first season with Long Island is just the third in which the Sharks have fielded a Division I hockey squad.

"Many of the established teams in college hockey play in honor of their culture and traditions, while we have the opportunity to create our own here at LIU," says Kostelecky. "We are able to lay the foundation of a successful program and develop our culture and traditions that will be passed to future generations. We also have the opportunity to achieve things that have never been done here before, which is exciting and motivating."

This season, there are six NCAA Division I Independents. Like Long Island, most are relatively new to top-level college competition. Others like Alaska and Alaska-Anchorage operate in distant locations. Kostelecky is one of five former Hawks skating for these teams. Tucker Ness, Ethan Szmagaj, and Teddy Lagerback are all at Arizona State. Forward Quinn Rudrud is a freshman at Alaska. For good measure, Trevor Stewart is an Anchorage assistant.

Despite not having a conference, the Independents have made an impact on college hockey this season. Alaska is 15-9-2, including an impressive road win over Denver last month when the Pioneers were either #1 or #2 in the country, depending on the poll. Minnesota was #2 in both recognized polls when they lost at Arizona State on the day after Thanksgiving. That same day, Long Island celebrated a 3-2 victory against #12 Ohio State. It was the school's first win against both a ranked opponent and a team from the Big Ten.

"It also gave our program credibility in the college hockey world, proving that we can play with and beat any of the big-time programs," Kostelecky says. "A big mantra of our program is 'fun to play here, hard to play here.' Being on Long Island and so close to New York City, there are a lot of activities in the area that make life away from the rink enjoyable. On ice we have competitions in almost every drill, which makes practices intense, but very fun. This is a very physically and mentally challenging program, however. There is a lot of physical fitness testing along with our culture of blocking shots and being hard to play against."

The Sharks host Alaska this weekend, then travel to Fairbanks the week after. With the Nanooks on a four-game winning streak and having won 10 of their last 12, the Long Island-Alaska contests should provide as much intensity as most conference games throughout the college hockey world.

Meanwhile, Stewart and the Seawolves go to Long Island at the end of the month. Stewart's move to Anchorage this season came after a long and successful junior hockey coaching career in the NAHL. Now he is among a group of coaches, staff, and players at UAA resurrecting a program which went dormant in 2020 as an effect of both COVID-19 and significant preexisting financial challenges.

"This has been an incredible learning experience for everyone involved," Stewart says. "First of all, we have a staff of five with no experience in college hockey whatsoever. From scheduling, traveling, ordering equipment, and following NCAA and university guidelines, we seem to be learning on the fly, which has made it that much more exciting."

Whatever else happens this season, UAA hockey's comeback story included a special moment on October 1st: a season-opening home win against Western Michigan.

"Winning our first game in our relaunch versus Western Michigan was not completely unexpected," says Stewart, noting, "There was no way that they could prepare for us, because we didn't even know who we were. It was a great feeling getting that first win for Coach [Matt] Shasby and all the players and alumni."

The geographic issues of playing outside the continental United States are a permanent reality for the Seawolves and their Fairbanks-based rivals. In the current college hockey world, that may make DI-Independent status the best – and possibly the only – option for now.

For UAA to remain viable, selling other programs on the value of a trip to The Last Frontier will likely be crucial.

"Everyone understands the time and financial obligations which are involved in traveling to Alaska to play college hockey games," Stewart acknowledges. "However, the experience that teams are able to carve out for themselves can far outweigh any negative aspects of playing up here."

At the moment, remote geography may also contribute to Arizona State's place among the ranks of the Independents. However, the Sun Devils don't have any shortage of opponents willing to travel to Tempe, at least during the early months of the season. Besides Minnesota, visitors in 2022/23 have also included Boston College and Minnesota State, plus an October matchup on neutral (but relatively close) ice in Las Vegas.

"The weather is a big change in the best way!" says Ness, who has played in 17 games as a freshman. "My roommates and I take scooters to the rink every morning, so we like to take advantage of the good weather whenever we can."

Whether taking the ice in the Valley of the Sun or in a place where the sun doesn't rise during the depths of winter, players on teams without a conference know there is not a conference tournament at the end of the season. An automatic NCAA Tournament bid is not available. There is nothing to bail out an otherwise underperforming team that gets hot at the right time. The already narrow path into the field of 16 is all-but closed to college hockey's Independents.

"One thing that makes not being in a conference special is how important every game is towards our end goal," Ness says. "We try to focus on just playing to our own standard instead of rankings, but not being in a conference makes us almost have to treat every game like our Super Bowl."

For the 13-18-0 Sun Devils, an NCAA Regional bid next month would be hard to imagine. That outcome is also unlikely for 11-15-1 Long Island.

"As a third-year program, a big focus for us is progress from previous years. This allows us to see growth year after year – through any ups and downs – regarding where we stand in the college hockey landscape," says Kostelecky, who echoes Ness regarding the NCAA postseason: "The only way into the National Tournament for us is to win as many games as possible. This makes each game much more intense and valuable for us."

Another common theme for those associated with college hockey's Independent programs is a forward-looking mindset and the idea that today's effort genuinely makes a difference in what happens tomorrow.

"The word that comes to mind when recruiting to UAA has been opportunity. Heck, we have 10 or 11 freshman that play every night and get a regular shift," says Stewart.

“Our players can step out of their apartments and take in the views of the Chugach Mountains. We are two miles away from the ocean…Our schedule is only going to get stronger, and our team should only get stronger. The future can be very bright for UAA Hockey.”

On the other side of the continent, Kostelecky shares a comparable outlook.

“By the time I graduate, I would like LIU to be a respected program in college hockey for our winning culture both on and off the ice. I would also like to see growth in the popularity of the program throughout Long Island and make Northwell Health Ice Center a tough place to play for our opponents.”

Results in 2022/23 suggest that Division I Independents are already offering tough opposition, even for some of college hockey’s most renowned programs.

Open Market for Waterloo Alumni

Former Hawks Gradually Enter New NIL Landscape

Black Hawks alumni shared their insights into name, image, and likeness compensation for waterlooblackhawks.com on March 13, 2024.

If you happen to be in Central Minnesota, take a second look at any hockey players you happen to see pictured in local advertising.

If you notice a tall, sturdy defenseman with familiar features, it might be Cooper Wylie. The sophomore at St. Cloud State has reached an agreement with CentraCare to license his image. CentraCare includes ten hospitals, dozens of clinics, and provides a wide variety of medical services. Their arrangement with Wylie is a small piece of the Name, Image, and Likeness (NIL) tidal wave sweeping through college sports since the summer of 2021.

"I have had a few opportunities [for] my photos to be used for advertising purposes," Wylie said via direct message. "I would be open for more NIL opportunities in the future."

It's not just big companies making deals with athletes. For a fan who would like to order a Michigan State sweatshirt with "Spartans" on the front and Patrick Geary's #2 on the back, now it's easy to find. Need Notre Dame goaltender Jack Williams to send a personalized video birthday greeting to a friend? That's available on a web page just a few clicks away from FightingIrish.com. Paying Arizona State defenseman Ethan Szmagaj for an autograph – which might have triggered an NCAA investigation a decade ago – can be done with a couple of clicks and a major credit card. And through the liberalization of NIL rules, some other opportunities are clearly now within bounds for players willing to put in the time.

However, NIL isn't for everyone. Not yet anyway. At least eight former Black Hawks contacted for this story indicated they had not pursued their NIL options or that they had nothing available.

Wylie's St. Cloud State teammate Mason Reiners has looked at NIL from a respectful distance. Reiners doesn't spend much time on social media, so video shoutouts or bespoke Instagram posts don't seem like a good fit.

"For me personally, I don't know if it will ever be something I really get into," says Reiners, adding, "I'm personally a fan of NIL. I think it's great that college athletes can take advantage of their own image and get something in return. I know several of my teammates have had deals over the last few years that have worked out great for them."

Wylie, Reiners, and other Huskies players have access to Opendorse. It is among the leading platforms in the NIL world, providing a high degree of standardization for schools across the country and covering all manner of college sports. While Opendorse is easily searchable by team or athlete, competitor INFLCR keeps their roster of NIL athletes behind a virtual wall. To see who might be open to a deal at Denver, Michigan, or Penn State, fans and companies alike need to register with that school's marketplace.

At least one quarter of Waterloo alumni playing college hockey have an active profile on the Opendorse platform. That includes Quinn Rudrud, who is skating at Augustana during the Sioux Falls school's first year on ice.

"As a first year Division I program, there aren't a whole lot of opportunities for NIL that have surfaced," Rudrud concedes. "Everyone is still learning what works best and how to navigate NIL deals…As times pass, I'm sure there will be much more development."

When it comes to learning about NIL, Rudrud says Augustana athletics leadership has been mindful to keep athletes from getting in over their heads.

"We have an admin at Augustana that helps us with NIL opportunities that come across a site that is secure for us called 'ARMS' in Opendorse. Anything and everything that goes through that site is overseen by administrators."

Meanwhile at Clarkson, Emmett Croteau has taken an active approach, even with the limited time he has available to spend on the site. The freshman goalie says the Opendorse universe is ripe for athletes who want to explore. Instead of waiting for businesses to reach out to him regarding endorsements, Croteau has been watching for products which align with his interests.

"They'll post themselves [on the site]. What they're about. What they're paying. What they want in return. What their product is. And it's just as simple as pressing 'apply.' They review your profile and then you're working together. It makes things pretty simple."

Croteau says he has made connections with clothing brands, vitamin suppliers, and a company working on sleep and mindfulness techniques. He credits his initial orientation with the platform for helping broaden the experience.

"When we came in, they're just like, 'Hey, there's this company we're partnering with. If you want to, you can sign up.' Once we signed up, we had a Zoom call with the company [Opendorse] going over the ins and outs of the app."

The current environment might also be helping to spur innovation and entrepreneurship in the Golden Knights' locker room. Some of Croteau's teammates are on the verge of forming their own business.

"They created a formula for hydration. It's an all-natural, fruit-based hydration mix…they've created something that's (one) healthy and (two) tastes pretty good," Croteau explains. "They've been building over the past two semesters and they're actually starting up their launch right now. So that's something cool to be a part of."

Across the state at Union College, Jacob Jeannette hasn't been paid for his image or his autographs. However with athletes now comfortably using their notoriety, Jeannette has no concerns about the side project he has chosen to pursue. Working with a web-based company called The Hockey Path, Jeannette provides video analysis and Zoom-based mentorship to a pair of U10 youth hockey teams in New York City.

"I found out about The Hockey Path through my teammate, Cole Kodsi," says Jeannette. "Being a broke college student, I wasn't about to pass up an opportunity to make some money, and also to teach the next generation of kids playing hockey."

Although the connection is virtual, Jeannette notes that he had prior firsthand experience coaching youth players at home in Duluth. During summers there, he works hockey camps with kids who are the same age and filled with the same adrenaline and love for the game.

Even before 2021, coaching youth athletes should generally have been permissible within the NCAA's amateurism requirements. Still, the new rules put Jeannette's mind at ease as he and more than 25 other college athletes appear on The Hockey Path coaching roster.

"I think because of the NIL rules, it definitely alleviates some pressure off me and all other players working with The Hockey Path as to the grey area around making money playing college sports."

Jeannette, Croteau, Wylie, and other former Hawks aren't seeing life-altering paychecks from their NIL arrangements and side hustles. Still, they are generally optimistic that the expanding ecosystem will be beneficial to themselves and the future players who will be on the ice in the years to come.

"You started to see all these big football players, big basketball players making these deals, seeing them on commercials," Croteau remembers, "Then it started to tumble its way down the ranks of Division I sports, and even Division III sports are taking part in this [now]. It's a very unique opportunity. People have stuff that they want to promote, and if we can help them, they're willing to give us some compensation. So yeah, it's a really cool opportunity."

McAdam Joins New League

Heads to Vegas for 3ICE Debut

A three-on-three summer hockey league opened in 2022; Eamon McAdam shared his thoughts on waterlooblackhawks.com June 15th.

Eamon McAdam might get some answers this weekend.

The former Waterloo Black Hawks goaltender will be part of a new summer hockey league which takes the ice for the first time on Saturday in Las Vegas. 3ICE will include stops in NHL cities like Denver, Pittsburgh, and Nashville before the schedule wraps up in late August. Among the unique aspects of this new circuit, games will be played three-on-three, like an extended overtime. The six participating teams are each coached by a former NHL star. They will meet in a playoff-like bracket every weekend.

McAdam knows all that. What he doesn't know is exactly how he was picked to be the goalie for Larry Murphy's squad.

"I'm actually interested to ask that question to Larry," McAdam says. "I've spoken to him a few times over e-mail…but I'm interested to see why he did pick me. It's always kind of interesting to see how people look at hockey and stats, and if they've seen you some time prior…I haven't been told why I stood out of the crowd."

News that McAdam had been selected for Murphy's seven-member team was not totally out-of-the-blue. This spring, the 27-year-old was playing in Denmark when he first heard about 3ICE.

"My agent reached out to me and said there was an opportunity with this new startup league, and it could be some really good publicity. I was in-season, so I wasn't able to make the tryout dates, but there was still an opportunity to put my name on the list and hope that I got picked off of a resume alone. Then I got a phone call towards the end of the regular season and was told that I was drafted."

McAdam's background is similar to many of the other 3ICE players. He made his Waterloo debut in January of 2011 and was 30-18-3 with two shutouts by the time he played his final junior game in 2013. That record does not include being named the competition's top goalie when Waterloo traveled to the 2012 Junior Club World Cup. McAdam's time with the

Hawks led to being drafted by the New York Islanders in the summer of 2013.

From the Cedar Valley, McAdam moved on to Happy Valley and three winters at Penn State. Signing his first pro contract in the spring of 2016, the Philadelphia area netminder covered a lot of ground in the seasons that followed: Bridgeport, Toronto, Binghamton, and Lehigh Valley in the AHL, plus Missouri, Worcester, Newfoundland, Adirondack, and Jacksonville in the ECHL. This season was his first in Europe.

With the 40ish other 3ICE players, there is a fair chance the group has collectively played in every active AHL and ECHL city at some point, with a smattering of NHL experience mixed in too. For McAdam, 3ICE means a reunion with a couple of former teammates.

"Griffin Molino – who I believe played in the USHL at some point [with Sioux Falls and Muskegon] – I had known him from back at New York Islanders camps, and then I played with him in Toronto," McAdam remembers. "I'm in the same boat with a guy named Chris Mueller, who was a bit older, a Michigan State guy, but he was also on the team in Toronto when I was there."

Players at every level of the game, from youth to the NHL, typically participate in some form of summer hockey, but McAdam knows this experience will be different.

"Usually you're getting into the gym and you're putting your work in on the ice to train, but it's just not quite the same. It's always different when you get on the ice, and that first puck drops. You take it to a whole different level, so to try and keep that intensity throughout the summer, it's going to be a bit of a learning curve."

The three-on-three format of 3ICE will give skilled forwards and defensemen plenty of room to show off their offensive abilities. McAdam and his fellow goalies will also have plenty of opportunity, although based on three-on-three overtimes during recent seasons, plus special events like the NHL All-Star Game, the success rate is likely to be lower for any goalie in the format.

"It's supposed to be a really fast, flowing league," says McAdam. "It's going to be very quick paced, and – I'm sure – high scoring, which obviously doesn't really play into my wheelhouse as a goalie, but that's part of it and I'm just happy to be a part of it.

"I've always found myself to be a little bit more of an athletic and crazy goalie in the net, so I think maybe it actually might play in my favor. You're not probably expected to make a ton of saves, but then if you have a really good outing when you're super dialed in, it might stand out."

McAdam may have to rely on himself to a greater degree in the 16-

minute matchups. Not only will he have fewer teammates to help protect then net, there also will be less time to build a rapport with them.

"We're going to fly out on a Friday and get a practice in with the team," McAdam noted about the schedule which will repeat itself weekend after weekend, "And then Saturday is game day."

After so much time in pro hockey, there are several destinations McAdam is looking forward to, even with a whirlwind travel schedule. He says he has never been to Vegas, but there are a few other stops he knows well, like Hershey, Pennsylvania, near his hometown.

"[And] London, Ontario, is right outside of where my girlfriend is from, so it's great. I'll get to catch up with her family and spend time with them. I'm thrilled to have a big crowd for that one. And Nashville is always a good time."

With his summer schedule aligned to the game schedule, plus the work needed for a goalie to play at a high level, McAdam has had plenty to think about, and that has meant a different level of attention regarding next fall and whether he will be back in Europe or elsewhere.

"It's a little bit up in the air. I've had a few looks with different teams, but I'm just trying to keep the door open."

As McAdam already learned by being picked to play in 3ICE, you never know who's watching or when you might have the chance to impress them.

Brandon Montour, Summer Play-Cation

A summer lacrosse championship showed Brandon Montour's versatility. He talked about it in the November 2014 One-Timer Digest.

Three months after playing for a national championship with the Waterloo Black Hawks, Brandon Montour found himself in nearly the same situation.

Identical, except that the team, the sport, and the country were different.

In late May, the Indiana Ice narrowly edged the Hawks for the Tier I junior hockey championship of the United States in a five-game series. Despite coming up one win short for the Clark Cup, Montour led the USHL with 16 playoff points.

By the latter half of August, Montour was in Langley, British Columbia, with the Six Nations Arrows bidding for the Minto Cup, the trophy presented to the junior lacrosse champion of Canada.

"I wasn't going to play this past summer," Montour notes, but "...my friends and the coaching staff there kept bugging me, saying, 'Hey, come play, come play.' I knew that we've had a legitimate chance of winning the national championship for the last three years, and we've come up short just by a game or two. I knew this year would be my last shot at it."

In 2011, Montour had helped another Six Nations team to Canada's Junior B title. As the potential missing piece, he joined the Arrows with the playoffs already underway and helped the team win the Ontario Championship, setting up a best-of-seven series for the Minto Cup – representative of Canadian lacrosse excellence for more than a century – against the Western Canadian champion Coquitlam Adanacs.

"There used to be a round robin with a number of teams, but they changed it up this year where the Ontario team plays the team that wins out of British Columbia and Alberta," Montour explains. "It turned out to be a very good series."

Just seconds into the first period of Game One, Montour scored the first goal of the finals. However, Coquitlam edged Six Nations 7-6, then won the second game of the series, 11-6. The Arrows fired back, running the floor at the Langley Event Center, winning an up-tempo Game Three by

14 goals before taking the next two contests by closer margins.

On the brink of clinching the series in the sixth game, Six Nations held a 6-5 lead after two periods. The Arrows emphatically claimed the trophy for the second time since 2007 with an eight-goal third. Montour notched one of the eight late goals during the 14-8 decision, finishing the finals with four goals and four assists.

"It was really special, and winning that with those guys – we played together since we were little, so I mean just years and years of practicing and playing together – the championship that we won was probably one of the toughest ever to win in lacrosse, so to win that with those guys was definitely huge," reflects Montour.

A life-altering moment on the other side of the continent makes it likely that Game Six of the Minto Cup series was the last meaningful lacrosse match in which Montour will play.

Between skating for the Hawks and dashing around the field for the Arrows, another team staked their claim to the athletic 20-year-old during June's NHL Draft in Philadelphia.

"Throughout the year, the [NHL] teams would come up and talk," says Montour, whose spectacular first season in Waterloo led to recognition as the USHL Player of the Year.

"Eventually I got an advisor and we got more into the NHL stuff leading up to the draft. After the season ended, I went out to Boston and trained for two or three weeks before the draft and kept getting phone calls and phone calls and heard rumors of where I was going to go in the draft, but I didn't really know for sure."

The waiting wasn't quite over on Day Two of the draft, but a glance at the Anaheim Ducks table foreshadowed what would happen next.

"I knew a few [Anaheim] guys from just throughout the year talking to me after the games," says Montour, "and they gave me the 'thumbs up.' I kind of had a gut feeling that that was where I was going to be picked."

With the 55th overall selection, Montour was washed into a whirlwind of hugs, handshakes, photographs, and interviews. Somewhere backstage, he had the chance to share the moment with Black Hawks teammate Mark Friedman, who was selected in the third round by the Philadelphia Flyers.

Eventually, Montour made his way upstairs in the Wells Fargo Center.

"Throughout the draft, every team had a suite so we'd go up to the suite and meet the coaching staff and the general manager and the owner to have food with them and have a greeting session before we got to training camp," Montour recalls.

Prospect camp was to begin sooner than Montour had expected.

"I drove from Boston to Philadelphia and then met my parents there [for the draft], so my plan was to go back to Boston and train for a week before training camp, but how Anaheim had it, they had camp…a day or two days after the draft," says Montour.

"Right from being picked and going to meet the coaching staff, I went back to the hotel room and packed up, and we left and went home right away. It was about a six- or seven-hour drive home, and then I packed up that night and kind of celebrated with my family and friends that were home, and took off the next day to Anaheim."

Montour made a strong impression in Anaheim. He was left with one, as well.

"Seeing their arena and dressing room, putting on their gear for practice and stuff like that, it was just an unbelievable feeling, and I can't wait to really get another taste."

A return to the Black Hawks is one step toward that goal. Future experience on the horizon with the University of Massachusetts Minutemen should also help him to get back to the Ducks' dressing room. And although Montour has put away his lacrosse stick and permanently swapped his sneakers for skates, raising the Minto Cup has its place too in his journey toward the NHL.

Annett Hoping for Christmas in July

Michael Annett reached stock car racing's highest levels after playing for the Black Hawks. He won a NASCAR Xfinity Series event at Daytona International Speedway in 2019. The Iowa native shared his thoughts for this waterlooblackhawks.com article dated July 27, 2018.

During the racing season, former Waterloo Black Hawks defenseman Michael Annett doesn't get home to Des Moines too often.

The skater-turned-stock car racer is guaranteed two trips to central Iowa when the NASCAR Xfinity Series makes its way to Iowa Speedway each summer. The second of those races is Saturday night in Newton, and besides turning laps at 130 miles per hour, Annett is looking forward to familiar scenery.

"One of my favorite parts is just going to your favorite restaurants; being able to go to those places and get comfort food. It just makes the whole weekend a lot more fun," Annett says, also noting that the holidays might be his next chance to catch up with many of the people he will be seeing.

"I moved down to North Carolina a little over ten years ago, and they're just not able to make it to a lot of races, but it's pretty easy to go up I-80 to Newton, and it's just fun for them to see what I do on a weekly basis."

Annett has been living away from home dating back to when he was still lacing up skates rather than racing up straightaways. Like many aspiring hockey players, Annett's efforts to pursue his dream literally took him far from family and friends. In high school, he moved to the Chicago suburbs to play for Team Illinois, then came to Waterloo for the 2003/04 and 2004/05 seasons.

That experience proved valuable when Annett switched pursuits.

"If you're going to be a professional in this sport, you've got to move down to the Mooresville/Charlotte area. You're getting thrown to the wolves at a young age if you want to be a race car driver, and I think the same thing goes if you want to be a professional hockey player," notes the 32-year-old.

"I had dealt with the move, dealt with being away from family and friends, and making new friends and making a new home at 16. When new guys move down here, I can see it. They're dealing with being away from home, and I already had about three years of that in me, so I pretty much was able just to focus on the job at hand. It's definitely helped me."

A few other hockey habits have also followed Annett into racing.

"Everybody that was on the Black Hawks back when I was would agree: you got on the bus, you played cards, you went to Fazoli's, and then you got back on the bus, and you went to sleep until we showed up at the rink.

"I've told everybody, I eat pasta when I'm at the track on Saturday afternoon, but my body tells me that I have to go to sleep afterwards, just because that's what I was trained to do. You eat pasta and you go to sleep, then you wake up and you get after it."

Saturday night, Annett is hoping the right balance of carbs and ethanol gasoline can help boost him toward the Xfinity Playoffs.

"Right now we're on the outside looking in as far as the playoffs go, and it's clear as day what we need to do week-in and week-out. That starts with just putting a whole weekend together: qualifying better, getting segment points, and having a great result at the end to make as many points as we can," he explains, adding, "I think we're just doing everything we can to right the ship and turn everything around and get ourselves into the playoffs."

The 2018 season started with near simultaneous hope and disappointment. Annett qualified 7th at Daytona – a track which has been friendly over the years – but a wreck in the second half of the race led to a 37th-place finish, his worst of the year. That has left the #5 JR Motorsports team playing from behind ever since.

Annett is as clear-eyed about his career on NASCAR's national circuits as he is about the 2018 season.

"I definitely thought I would have won more races than I have, and the plan is to win a whole lot more races. I signed a two-year extension with JR Motorsports and there's definitely still time to get it done, but more pressure than anybody ever could put on me, I put on myself.

"I'm fortunate that I get two more years at least, and the rest of this season, to accomplish those goals. Right now, I'd say I was disappointed with the results I've had in 10-plus years, but I'm also able to still shift and get those results."

The contract will keep Annett employed by the Earnhardt family, owners of JR Motorsports. It's not the first time he has driven for racing royalty after being on teams owned by Richard Petty and Rusty Wallace earlier in his career.

"All those names that you mentioned, they're the first ones to try to make you better as a driver, so I've been very fortunate to have those people."

Besides owners, Annett has teammates he can lean on. JR Motorsports driver Elliott Sadler is currently third in the Xfinity standings, and Justin Allgaier won at Iowa when the series stopped in Newton earlier this summer.

"We've got a lot of notes in our notebook and we'll probably unload right where he left that car in victory lane, so it's very beneficial to be with a team like JR Motorsports and have all that feedback," Annett says.

If Annett can make the most of that information and take the checkered flag for the first time Saturday night in Iowa, it will certainly spark a celebration among the dozens of family, friends, and fans who will be on hand.

It's even possible that party still might be going on when Annett finds his way back to Iowa for Christmas.

[Postscript – In February 2019, Annett won a NASCAR Xfinity series race at Daytona.]

Stressful Summers of the 70s

Lean Years Led to New Opportunities

This article first appeared on waterlooblackhawks.com in July, 2025.

Waterloo Black Hawks fans had to sweat through several summers in the 1970s. When the ice melted at McElroy Auditorium in the spring, it wasn't always clear whether the Hawks – or the ice – would be back when cooler weather arrived.

"This is a matter of salvaging a hockey team," said Joe Nutting in June of 1973. Nutting was a director of Northeast Iowa Sports, Inc., one of the entities which operated the Black Hawks during that period. He and other Waterloo residents repeatedly grappled with the challenge of keeping hockey from being scrapped during an era of change.

The Black Hawks had two opportunities to play for a championship between 1973 and 1977. Three other times during that span, the organization faced possible bankruptcy. Over the same timeframe, the United States Hockey League started every new season with a different collection of teams. Uncertainties shadowed the USHL and the Black Hawks during the 1970s. Despite that – or perhaps because of it – the league and the team adapted and evolved toward 21st century success.

The venue known as McElroy Auditorium – and today, called the Hippodrome – stands prominently on the National Cattle Congress grounds. It was operated through a partnership between the NCC and City of Waterloo for more than a decade before a major renovation in 1962. An ice plant and rink infrastructure were part of the upgrades, creating the situation necessary for Waterloo to join the USHL. The Black Hawks won five championships in the 60s, attracting a passionate following. Northeast Iowa Sports was the non-profit in charge of the team's business operations. Its directors were prominent figures in the Cedar Valley business community, and each season, a different executive or entrepreneur would serve as board president.

By the early 1970s, expansion had more than doubled the size of the National Hockey League, and other pro leagues grew to match. Senior players had once been attracted to Waterloo by the combination of high-level hockey and fulltime off-ice employment. The number of swift-skating, hard-hitting college graduates or tradesmen – previously with better prospects for career success off the ice than on it – shrank. There were more chances to "make it" in pro hockey than there had ever been, but Waterloo and the USHL were a long way from the NHL or the newly-created World Hockey Association. At McElroy Auditorium, wins were harder to earn, crowds were marginally smaller, and expenses increased with road destinations farther away than they had been in the prior decade.

During the 1972/73 season, the Hawks were a solid 23-18-1. Nonetheless, they placed third in their division and outside the four-team postseason field. Waterloo still hosted the two-game divisional playoff series between the Chicago Warriors and Green Bay Bobcats; a combined total of 1,306 neutral fans attended. Had the Hawks skated in those games, ticket sales would likely have been several times larger, and might have limited Northeast Iowa Sports' losses for the season. Instead, Waterloo hockey finished the fiscal year with a budget gap of over $21,000, an amount which would have purchased five new 1973 Chevy Cameros at sticker price with enough left over to keep them gassed up at approximately 40 cents per gallon.

A spring pledge drive helped assure that Northeast Iowa Sports would be able to cover its losses. Eighty people committed to contributing up to $400 apiece to keep hockey going. However, those pledges were never collected. Converting the team into a for-profit venture with local investors seemed like a better way forward. The newly-organized Black Hawk Enterprises Inc. was created to pay off the debt and make arrangements for the 1973/74 season.

"What it boils down to is that we will have strong financial backing from a few but still leave it open for community investment," said Nutting. "The major operation will be left up to the biggest spenders."

Black Hawk Enterprises immediately had 35 investors, many who had played significant roles during the non-profit years. By mid-July, 71 shareholders bought in, generating $30,000 from a stock sale. They hoped to make a profit from hockey, but at minimum they accepted the personal financial risks of keeping the team active.

Meanwhile, the Soo Canadians of Sault Ste. Marie, Ontario, had been part of the USHL since 1969. After four years of middling to poor results, they dropped out. The league still managed to expand to nine teams in the summer of 1973, adding new clubs in Milwaukee and Madison. The schedule was stretched from 42 to 48 games, providing optimism to Waterloo investors that shorter road trips and three additional home games could provide a financial tailwind. The league also considered the intriguing possibility of a collaboration with the WHA. USHL leaders began discussing overtures to the upstart major league circuit as early as September.

The Thunder Bay Twins were eventually the 1973/74 regular season champions. They followed up with a playoff title, sweeping the Black Hawks during a three-game Final series. Even so, the Twins were one of the teams considered to be in poor financial condition ahead of the league's May 1974 meeting. Chicago and the Copper Country Chiefs of Calumet, Michigan, were also struggling. The Madison Blues were worst off. After one season, Madison owed the USHL $3,000 in back fees. They could not provide the league with the required $7,000 guarantee that they would play their slated games in 1974/75. Blues ownership and USHL officials spent months trying to work out a solution, with the league schedule delayed as a result. Madison's players were finally dispersed to other clubs in mid-August, including a new team in Stevens Point, the Central Wisconsin Flyers.

Hopes to affiliate with the WHA were also quashed after a nearly yearlong flirtation.

"The WHA board of governors voted against a formal tieup between the major professional league and one of North America's leading amateur circuits," the *Waterloo Courier* reported on June 23rd. "[It] would have called upon WHA members to provide the USHL teams with around seven players a year and financial support based on the development and eventual progress of these players into professional hockey."

For its own part, the USHL rejected a counteroffer which would have allowed league teams to create individualized partnerships with WHA clubs. USHL leaders believed that would lead to a competitive imbalance if such deals weren't standardized.

In Waterloo, the Black Hawks enjoyed a relatively quiet summer in 1974. The team's push to the playoffs generated positive publicity and good crowds. Season attendance climbed to nearly 83,000, approximately 2,800 per game. First-year head coach Dave Swick was voted the USHL's Coach of the Year. Black Hawks Enterprises did not pay a dividend on its shares, but did well enough to invest in McElroy Auditorium improvements. When hockey returned in the fall, new plastic dasherboards and glass were installed to replace the plywood half walls and wire screens which had been in place for years.

The Hawks did well again in 1974/75, posting a 30-15-3 regular season record. During the 1975 playoffs, Waterloo earned a rematch in the championship series against Thunder Bay. The Twins prevailed again, this time in four games. However, Waterloo benefitted from the additional revenue created from four postseason home games. In the 1975 offseason, the team focused on organizing a pro shop to serve the larger Cedar Valley hockey community and youth program. The big news that summer was the creation of the Columbus High School team and the Waterloo Warriors to represent the city's public high schools.

Other USHL organizations faced a more tenuous offseason. After winning the league title, Thunder Bay went on to claim the Allan Cup as Canada's senior national champions. Then they dropped out of the USHL, in part due to high travel costs from flying to all of their road games. Chicago left the league, and Copper Country vacillated all summer, just like Madison the year before. The Milwaukee Admirals had trouble securing home dates in a building they shared with the National Basketball Association's Milwaukee Bucks. The USHL did add the Traverse City Bays, but the new destination meant a long trip around Lake Michigan for almost all of the expansion club's opponents.

"It is hoped that Marquette [Michigan] will be able to revitalize their community hockey enthusiasm and support; and for Calumet and Central Wisconsin, the 75/76 season will either make or break their franchise operations," noted the *USHL Yearbook* in a remarkably candid preseason assessment.

A renaissance in those cities didn't happen.

Copper Country – who did not officially commit to playing in 75/76 until September – dropped out of the league before Christmas. Marquette and Central Wisconsin left the USHL after the 1975/76 season ended. Making matters worse, the USHL was forced to find a new commissioner in early November 1975 when 51-year-old Bob Kasubeck died of a heart attack.

The Black Hawks were also facing trouble as the 1975/76 season commenced. Season ticket sales were down. As of October 21st, the team was "...nearly 100 season tickets short of the 700 they sold last year. That's far below the goal of 850 that General Manager Jack Barzee established..." noted the *Waterloo Courier*. Black Hawks players were also dissatisfied. Several veterans refused, at least initially, to sign their contracts, even at or near the league maximum of $50 per game.

Results before Christmas were poor. A big finish allowed Waterloo to win 30 games for a second consecutive season and earn a playoff bid for the third straight year. Yet big crowds still did not materialize often enough during the 1976 portion of the schedule. Season attendance was off by an average of 650 fans per night. The difficult winter wiped out $14,000 in reserve funds which Black Hawks Enterprises had accumulated. Instead, the closing financial report showed a debt of nearly $23,000.

As the team reviewed the dire situation, a long-term investment of time and resources in the community's youth program paid off.

"Should the Black Hawks fold, hundreds of Waterloo and Cedar Falls kids would be without hockey for the first time in 14 years," wrote Richard Smith in a letter to the *Courier*. "At a time when the Junior Hawk program has become a success for both the kids and fans, and at a time when both the Columbus and public schools high school hockey teams have just completed their first year with a promising success, it seems ironic to abandon the hockey team that brought indoor skating to this area 14 years ago."

It was a broadly-held sentiment and helps explain why dozens of fans committed to sell season tickets for 1976/77 a month after the old schedule had ended. On May 15, Black Hawk Enterprises voted to prepare for another year. It was not clear who the Hawks would play.

Marquette and Central Wisconsin were out. Milwaukee and Traverse City both lost substantial sums, despite facing each other for the league championship. Green Bay accumulated $45,000 in debt, but the venerable Bobcats were committed to playing again. The Sioux City Musketeers made a small profit. USHL leadership hoped to stabilize the league through expansion. Madison, Peoria, Omaha, Des Moines, and Grand Rapids were all considered candidates. In the end, only Grand Rapids (the Blades) joined, despite geographic concerns ("If we can stay on this side of the lake, I think we have a chance," is how departing Black Hawks Enterprises President Dave Tyler had expressed the state of affairs earlier in the offseason).

The Admirals were given an extension into July of 1976 to commit to another season. They managed to solve their financial difficulties and signed on for another year. It was a mixed blessing. That summer, the NBA and ABA merged, again delaying Milwaukee's available home dates. That created a domino effect which stunted ticket sales opportunities in other USHL markets. The league schedule wasn't finalized until August 30th.

Waterloo opened the 1976/77 campaign with an 8-2 road loss against the Blades. By the end of November, the Hawks had only won twice. It was unfortunate timing for the club to have a season which – by some measures – was the worst in team history up to that point. The 20-28-0 Hawks missed the playoffs again and lost $26,000 in the process. A month after the schedule ended, stockholders met and voted to sell the club, placing an ad in *The Hockey News*.

Other USHL teams fared just as badly, regardless of record. An April 1977 estimate put the collective losses of the league clubs at a quarter million dollars. By this point, the USHL's other teams each had small ownership groups or individual owners. Gary Lipschutz was among them. The founder of the Sioux City Musketeers had also become president of the USHL. It was Lipschutz who came to the Black Hawks' rescue in June. After multiple potential deals to sell the Black Hawks had fallen through, the league itself pledged to support the team during the 1977/78 season.

"The USHL has arranged a series of loan guarantees to be sure the Black Hawks will operate this year," Lipschutz said at the end of June. "Waterloo is a good hockey town, and the league needs Waterloo. We feel things will be turned around here."

He went on to make a further optimistic prediction which proved true in ways he couldn't have imagined that summer.

"The caliber of hockey in this league is going to continue to improve. The talent available is getting better. Several higher leagues have folded and the possible merger (between the National Hockey League and World Hockey Association) would make more money available for development. We'd try to get our share of that money."

Another hockey merger made local news in late August. The Milwaukee Admirals defected to the International Hockey League, leaving Sioux City, Green Bay, and Waterloo as the only clubs officially committed to the USHL for the coming season. The Midwest Junior Hockey League was also down to three members: the Austin Mavericks, St. Paul Vulcans, and Bloomington Jr. Stars. An agreement to bring the six teams together into one league was quickly approved. The former MJHL clubs would continue to play with all-junior rosters. The Hawks, Musketeers, and Bobcats would feature a limited number of senior players during a three-year transition period (later reduced to two seasons).

"I was really down on it when we first started talking about the idea," Barzee frankly revealed when asked about the situation at that time, "But now I see that things will work out better than they did before...There's advantages of using junior players. The Midwest Junior League has really been instrumental in developing young American hockey players. And, if you have players drafted (by the National Hockey League), you'll get development money for them."

The transition was long in Waterloo. In the immediate aftermath, the Black Hawks won championships in 1978 and 1979. However, a good all-junior season in 1979/80 coupled with poor financial results convinced Barzee to relocate to Dubuque. Waterloo again scrambled to stay in the USHL for the sake of youth and high school hockey programs. The hockey community clawed through the 1980s and 90s with only a few successful years. Winning records, big crowds, and the development pipeline Lipschutz and Barzee anticipated truly began to emerge in the 2000s.

The USHL and the Waterloo Black Hawks persevered and became part of the success stories for hundreds of individual players. It couldn't have happened without determination and creativity during the warm, worrisome summers of the 1970s.

Where Are They Now: Bill Bennett

With hockey halted by the COVID-19 pandemic, Bill Bennett shared his memories of being a Black Hawk during the 1970s in an article for waterlooblackhawks.com on April 17, 2020.

When the Black Hawks took the ice for the final time this spring on March 11th against the Dubuque Fighting Saints, 6-foot, 2-inch Patrick Guzzo lined up for the opening faceoff. Xander Lamppa – just an inch shorter – was at his left. The starting lineup also included 6-foot, 1-inch defenseman Mason Reiners and 6' 2" goalie Gabriel Carriere. On the Waterloo bench, Joe Cassetti, Ondrej Psenicka, Brehdan Engum, and Jacob Bengtsson all stood 6' 3" or taller.

The landscape was far different in the fall of 1974 when 6-foot, 6-inch, 21-year-old Bill Bennett joined the Hawks. At that time, he was the biggest player in the United States Hockey League, and there weren't many others who were close.

"Now I would be normal-sized, but back then, I used to get all those comments, like 'Why aren't you playing basketball,'" Bennett remembers. "I didn't know I was going to be 6-6 when I was a kid."

Bennett did know that he was growing up in a hockey family. His father – Harvey – had a long career as a goalie in the 1940s and 50s, including a brief stint in the NHL with the Boston Bruins. His older brothers took to the game and went on to success in college, then later made their way into the pros. By 1974, Curt Bennett was becoming one of the top forwards for the Atlanta (today Calgary) Flames.

With the 1974/75 hockey season approaching, Bill Bennett was invited to Atlanta's camp with his brother. The Flames directed Bill to the Des Moines Capitols of the International Hockey League. After just a few IHL appearances, the big forward was relocated to Waterloo, joining the Black Hawks for games at McElroy Auditorium by early November.

Bennett says his opportunity in the old senior-level USHL helped him gain confidence. The physicality of the league played to his strengths.

"My dad basically said, 'You're 6-6, you better act it.'"

Beyond helping him on the ice, his size was also an asset at a time when Black Hawks players were employed at regular jobs during the day.

"I worked at a place called Peterson Seed. I'll never forget I used to have to be at work at 7 o'clock in the morning, and I'd work until 4, and we had practice at 5 every day. It was heavy work lifting seed bags from 50 to 150 pounds, which I sort of liked at that young age…it was very physical, then you'd have to practice, and I think it was good for me."

Bennett appeared in 34 games for Waterloo, scoring a couple of goals shortly after joining the team and finishing the season with four, plus seven assists. The Black Hawks were the USHL's South Division winners and went on the league championship series, falling to the Thunder Bay Twins for the second consecutive year. However, by the end of the schedule, Bennett was hurting. He would have several offseason hernia surgeries, which kept him off the ice as teams regrouped for the start of the 1975/76 season. When Bennett was ready to go, he found a place with another USHL club – the Central Wisconsin Flyers – and played a limited number of games that winter.

Nonetheless, for 1976/77, Bennett earned a home with the IHL's Columbus Owls and had a breakout season, opening up doors for future years in the American Hockey League.

"It usually took me two years to adjust to a league," Bennett recalls. "Things were starting to come together when I played in Columbus. I had a pretty good season there, and I ended up in Rochester in the American League at the end of the season, and then Boston signed me from that."

As a Rhode Island native, the Bruins had been the team Bennett cheered for during his childhood. It was also the organization where his father had been a netminder more than 20 years earlier. On December 12, 1978, Bennett had the chance to put on the gold and black "B" logo for the first time in an official game, with his first moments on the ice resulting in the situation that every player dreams of.

"It was three to five seconds into my first shift. I jumped the boards and skated to the net and scored. My dad was at the game, so that was great. I wish I had the film."

Not quite halfway through the first period, his goal was the first during a 7-3 Boston win against the Vancouver Canucks. During six additional games with the Bruins, Bennett notched another four assists. Although he spent much of that year in Rochester, Bennett had become the first former Black Hawk to make it from Waterloo to the pinnacle of professional hockey.

The next season, he joined New England's new NHL club, the Hartford Whalers. Although optimistic that the situation in Hartford might be a big opportunity, Bennett played in just 24 NHL games for the Whalers in 1979/80. They were his final appearances at hockey's highest level, and

Bennett retired in 1982 after two more minor league campaigns.

Since completing his playing career, Bennett has operated Bennett Sports – a hockey pro shop in Rhode Island – while also working as a commercial fisherman. Additionally, he still skates with the Boston Bruins Alumni Association, playing charity games throughout the northeast.

Bennett became reacquainted with the USHL a decade ago. In 2009, his nephew Mac joined the Cedar Rapids RoughRiders for a season, later attending Michigan and eventually retracing his uncle's footsteps to the AHL's Rochester Americans.

Speaking recently with waves in the background while harvesting clams, Bill Bennett reflected on his own climb in the sport.

"As you go up, the guys…I don't think they're as close. When I was in Waterloo, I'd say there were about ten of us, every day, we were always together doing something, but as you go up the ladder, there's less and less, guys go on their own. But back then, everybody was in basically the same boat."

The camaraderie of Black Hawks players hasn't changed much in the 45 years since Bennett came to Waterloo. Today's players are just a little younger…and on average, a little taller than most of Bennett's teammates.

Seals to Sharks with Waterloo in Between

Sommer Remembers Black Hawks Stop

This article appeared on waterlooblackhawks.com on April 24, 2020.

Roy Sommer appeared in three National Hockey League games.

He was a Waterloo Black Hawk for just slightly longer.

Both episodes were brief stops in a hockey playing and coaching career which has now extended through parts of six decades and brought Sommer back to the NHL last winter as associate coach of the San Jose Sharks.

Spending more than 40 years in the game professionally is impressive under any circumstances. Doing it as someone born in Northern California in the late 1950s – when the NHL had just six teams and the closest one was two time zones away – puts the feat in a different context.

"For the [California] kids today, there's a lot more exposure," Sommer says. "With mass media and everything else, it's a lot easier to get your name out now than it was back then. You had to have a little bit of luck, and someone had to find you."

The NHL expanded to California during Sommer's formative years with the founding of the L.A. Kings and the Oakland Seals in 1967. As a Bay Area native, the Seals' arrival was particularly significant for Sommer.

"I did a little bit of visiting stick boy stuff. Then, when someone would score a goal or there was a penalty, I would run in and give the information to a guy, and he would put it on a tickertape and send it all over the league…that was kind of the internet back then."

By the early 1970s, Sommer became a successful high school player looking for opportunities to develop beyond those available to him in the Golden State. He had to travel a thousand miles north to find his first big break.

"I was discovered to play juniors at a hockey school in Nelson, British Columbia. At the end of the two-week hockey school, we had a game on the weekend," recalls Sommer. "There happened to a scout in the stands the game I played – a guy named Wayne Myers that scouted for the Edmonton Oil Kings – he saw me and invited me to come to the Edmonton Oil King camp."

Although Sommer didn't land a spot with the Oil Kings, he found a home instead with the Spruce Grove Mets of the Alberta Junior Hockey League. Spruce Grove won the Centennial Cup as Canada's Junior A champions, opening the door for Sommer to an opportunity at the major junior level the next season, and eventually creating enough notoriety for the Toronto Maple Leafs to draft him in 1977.

At 20-years-old, and as a late-round pick, Sommer still had a big climb ahead of him when he joined the Saginaw Gears of the International Hockey League that fall. Making circumstances more challenging, that strong Gears team didn't have a place for him, setting up his brief sojourn with the Black Hawks.

"I was loaned out by Saginaw," says Sommer, "because I just wasn't playing a lot. They tried to get me some ice time. I think Jack Barzee must have called and said 'Hey, do you guys have any extra players,' and I think that's probably how I got loaned out there."

Barzee – the Black Hawks' head coach at the time – was in an interesting personnel situation during the autumn of 1977. In the offseason, the senior-level United States Hockey League had merged with the Midwest Junior Hockey League. The 1977/78 campaign was to include hybrid rosters with former USHL clubs being required to include a handful of juniors. Many of the league's older, established players either retired or left for other hockey opportunities. Sommer's age made him one of the youngest senior players, just outside of the junior category.

On and off the ice, he was paired on a forward line with Black Hawks veteran Dave Klingbeil, who brought a unique combination of scoring ability and toughness. Like Sommer, Klingbeil had gone far from home to pursue the game, playing college hockey at the University of Alaska after growing up in North Dakota.

"He would play hockey down there [in Waterloo] and go back to Alaska in the summer to work as a welder on the oil pipeline," Sommer remembers about his roommate.

During their brief time as linemates, Sommer and Klingbeil found chemistry quickly. Their most notable exploits came in a 5-4 come-from-behind overtime win against the Sioux City Musketeers on November 18, 1977. Klingbeil set up Sommer's game-tying goal with 54 seconds left in regulation; 36 seconds into overtime, Sommer recorded his third assist of the night on Klingbeil's game-winner.

A week later, Sommer was on his way back to Saginaw.

He moved around to a number of clubs in the next few years, making the most of several unique and timely experiences, none more so than a 1979 tryout with the U.S. Olympic Team. Even though Sommer didn't make Herb Brooks' squad, the experience later opened another door while Sommer was called up by the Houston Apollos in the Central Hockey League.

"I was supposed to be there for three games, and we ended up playing the Olympic team. I got a goal and an assist or something like that, and we were one of the only minor league teams to beat them, and instead of being in Houston for three games, I ended up staying there."

When the Edmonton Oilers moved their CHL farm club from Houston to Wichita the next year, Sommer went with. By January of 1981, he was brought up to Edmonton, making him one of the first California-born players to appear in the NHL. Sommer joined an Oilers team on the verge of becoming one of the greatest of their era.

"You could tell that whole organization was going to be good. Just a lot of really young, good, gifted kids."

Kids who would become future All-Stars and Hall of Famers like Jari Kurri, Mark Messier, Glenn Anderson, and Paul Coffey.

And there was a youngster named Wayne, not quite two years younger than the then-24-year-old Sommer.

"[Gretzky] was a little skinny guy, about 170 pounds," says Sommer.

The Great One and the forward from California played three games together. Sommer scored during his first night on NHL ice – a 9-1 win against the Montreal Canadiens – and was involved in a fight with another future Hall of Famer, defenseman Rod Langway.

Sommer was not there for Oilers' Stanley Cups in the years which followed. In fact, he had left the ice for the bench well before Edmonton won their fifth Cup in 1990.

Sommer began a long association with the Sharks after they became Northern California's new team. He served a couple of seasons in San Jose as an assistant before spending more than 20 years coaching the organization's top prospects in the American Hockey League.

His long tenure brought him into contact with an array of former Black Hawks: Eriah Hayes, James Marcou, Matt Fornataro, and Corey Quirk for full seasons with the Worcester Sharks. Many others for abbreviated stays there. For just a matter of weeks, Joe Pavelski was one of his charges before starting an All-Star career at the NHL level.

On his own "call up" to the Sharks' NHL staff this winter, Sommer reflects, "It was fun getting back to the NHL, but it's a different animal though, I'll tell you that, than the American League."

A different animal, perhaps, but nothing Sommer hasn't seen as the game has taken him from California, through Waterloo, and to places in every other direction on the compass.

A Year Without the Black Hawks

This story was written for the Black Hawks' 2009/10 yearbook.

"Be careful what you wish for."

"Sometimes blessings come in disguise."

These two clichéd phrases, with their opposing implications, could have bracketed the short history of professional hockey in Waterloo.

After five consecutive USHL championships in the 1960's, the Black Hawks had made hockey a sensation in the Cedar Valley. But with the United States Hockey League faltering, the sport, in an organized form, was on the verge of disappearing from the community less than a decade after arriving. The fledgling Minnesota North Stars appeared as saviors. In 1968/69, their minor league affiliate, the Memphis South Stars, lost $200,000. McElroy Auditorium, just a few hours' drive from the Met Center in Bloomington and home to thousands of passionate hockey fans, must have seemed an ideal spot for Minnesota to develop prospects. For many fans, cheering for the North Stars' top farm team must have seemed like an easy conversion.

Forty years ago, the Iowa Stars moved into Waterloo for the 1969/70 Central Hockey League season. At that time, the CHL was made up of seven clubs and stretched from Texas, through Oklahoma and Missouri, north to Nebraska and Iowa. Fort Worth was the farthest destination from Waterloo, over 800 miles away. Chicago, Detroit, Boston, St. Louis, New York, and Toronto had affiliates in the league, with each team playing a 72-game schedule.

Waterloo was the smallest city in the league, but at the outset, North Stars officials said they believed that was a good thing.

According to Minnesota president Walter Bush Jr., "the smaller size of this metropolitan area can be a plus, not a minus…it seems to us that it gives the organization and players a better chance to become part of the community."

John Muckler was the North Stars' choice to manage the operation. He became part of the Minnesota franchise after working as a player-coach, then later general manager in the Eastern Hockey League, a level similar to the old USHL. When the North Stars joined the NHL as an expansion team in 1967, Muckler was brought in to lead the South Stars front office in Memphis and later moved with the club to the Cedar Valley. After Waterloo, he would spend another decade in the minors before landing in the NHL as an assistant coach with the Edmonton Oilers. Muckler won five Stanley Cups there in various roles, then moved on to work for the Buffalo Sabres, New York Rangers, and Ottawa Senators as either head coach or general manager. He still draws a paycheck at the NHL level as a senior advisor to the Phoenix Coyotes.

Muckler's partner in Memphis and Waterloo was Head Coach Parker MacDonald. In the early 1950's, MacDonald arrived in the NHL as a forward with the Toronto Maple Leafs. He would end up eventually playing for four of the NHL's original six teams, having a career year in 1962/63 on a line with Gordie Howe. Minnesota selected him in the 1967 expansion draft, and transitioned him into a coaching role after a full season with the North Stars. Like Muckler, MacDonald would eventually climb into a head coaching role in "the show" with both Minnesota and the Los Angeles Kings.

Muckler and MacDonald enjoyed a successful debut at McElroy Auditorium in the Stars' first game on October 11, 1969. Jim Benzelock, one of only six Iowa Stars to never play in the NHL, scored the team's first goal 4:12 into the game. The Stars took their first lead on a Mike Chernoff score 12:33 into the second. Grant Erickson delivered the game-winner with 1:51 remaining, and Iowa held on for a 4-3 win against the Omaha Knights, an affiliate of the New York Rangers. A crowd of 3,192 piled into McElroy to see the game.

Although he didn't play, former Waterloo Black Hawk star goalie Jim Coyle dressed for the inaugural game, because Minnesota had only sent one net-minder to Iowa at that point. Twenty-year-old Gilles Gilbert was in net for 34 saves in the Stars' first game. He would be the club's regular goalie throughout the season, stacking up a 17-16-5 record in 39 appearances. Gilbert was also the Stars' player who would go on to perhaps the most notable NHL career, winning 192 games in parts of 14 big-league seasons. As a member of Boston Bruins, he was an NHL All-Star in 1974, picking up a career-high 34 wins that season, and back-stopping Boston to the Stanley Cup Final. He was also along for the ride in 1978 and 1979 when the Bruins returned to the championship series.

Gilbert's roommate in Waterloo was Minnesota's hottest prospect at that time. Dick Redmond was the North Stars' first round draft choice in 1969. The previous year for St. Catherine's in the Ontario Hockey Association, he had racked up 74 points, the most by a defenseman in that league since Bobby Orr. Redmond didn't mature into another Orr, but he did enjoy a solid NHL career, first appearing with the North Stars the same year he was in Waterloo. He would also play for the California Golden Seals, Chicago Blackhawks, Atlanta Flames, St. Louis Blues, and ended up as Gilbert's teammate again in Boston in time for the Bruins' trip to the 1979 Stanley Cup Final.

Nineteen other members of the Iowa Stars played in the NHL at some point. Of the six who didn't make it, three played in the World Hockey Association, the rival league in the 1970's which attracted stars like Howe and Bobby Hull near the end of their careers. When the circuit folded at the end of the decade, the remnant of the WHA was absorbed into the National Hockey League, much like the AFL into the NFL.

* * *

The victory in the season-opener was not a fluke. *Courier* Sports Editor Russ Smith dubbed the Stars the "rollicking, brawling, bad boys of the Central Hockey League," and the roughhousing style led to wins. The Stars stayed in the midst of a tight playoff race which went down to the final weekend of the season. With two games remaining, Iowa was two points behind Omaha and Tulsa with home games scheduled against Fort Worth and Oklahoma City.

Friday, March 22, 1970, it looked like the Stars would pick up a vital win against the Fort Worth Wings at McElroy. With a 3-2 lead in the closing minutes, Mike Chernoff appeared to seal the game with an empty net goal, but the play was called back because it had been set up by a two-line offside pass. The linesman who made the call was former Black Hawk Dave Swick.

The Wings scored the game-tying goal, and the contest finished in a 3-3 tie, effectively ending Iowa's chance for a regular season title. It took 15 minutes for Swick and the other officials to make it off the ice with debris from the stands raining down on them. Threatening phone calls, including suggestions that angry fans might bomb his house, convinced Swick to ask for police protection. It wouldn't be the last ugly ending for the Stars.

The club did win their final regular season game for a second place finish in the league. Chernoff, who would play in just one career NHL game, notched a goal and an assist to finish in a tie for the team scoring lead with captain Bill Orban, who had been temporarily called up to Minnesota. Both men ended up with 75 points. Other notable achievements belonged to Danny Seguin, who won most popular player voting among Waterloo fans. Dennis O'Brien finished as the CHL's penalty minute leader with 331 in 72 games.

The Stars began their first playoff series later that week against Toronto's affiliate, the Tulsa Oilers, and advanced in six games. The Jack

Adams Cup championship series opened against Omaha on April 8th with a 6-2 loss. Iowa rallied for a 3-1 win in Game Two, but the next three games were scheduled in Omaha. The Knights picked up a 4-2 victory, then a 7-6 overtime decision, which came in spite of a Chernoff hat trick.

Down three games to one in the best-of-seven series, Chernoff turned in another big play, giving Iowa a 5-4 lead midway through the third period of Game Five. As had been the case for Chernoff weeks earlier against Fort Worth and the night before in Omaha, the effort wasn't enough. The Knights scored three unanswered goals, two by future NHL journeyman Bert Wilson, to win the game and the series. For finishing second in the regular season and as runners-up in the playoffs, Iowa Stars players received $1,400 each, the equivalent of nearly $7,800 today. Winning the regular season title and the Adams Cup would have been worth another $400 per man.

Winning those championships would not have kept the Stars in Waterloo, however.

During 1969/70, an average of 2,100 fans filed into McElroy Auditorium for each game. The *Waterloo Courier* estimated that attendance for the season was more than the total population of the city and suggested that few other communities with a professional hockey team could boast about similar success. Unfortunately for the Stars, their attendance was still last in the Central Hockey League. The club made approximately $163,000 from ticket sales, well short of the $200,000 the North Stars had estimated in their budget. On the whole, the franchise lost $130,000 to $150,000.

A clue about one unrealized expectation may have been right in the team name: the Iowa Stars. The franchise believed fans from across Eastern Iowa, if not an even broader portion of the state, would be drawn to the action. A letter published in the Stars' game program from *Cedar Rapids Gazette* Sports Editor Gus Schrader predicted fans would "flock" up the Cedar River corridor.

Schrader wrote, "Certainly at least half the fans who see the Iowa Stars play this season will be from cities, towns, and rural areas outside the Waterloo-Cedar Falls metropolitan area... Waterloo merchants are going to be pleased if the fans develop the habit of coming to Waterloo."

The estimate was optimistic, and Iowa Stars hockey was not as habit-forming as hoped. The North Stars moved their top farm team to Cleveland before the fall of 1970, with a commitment from the private ownership there to share expenses. On the same day that decision was announced, Northeast Iowa Sports, the organization overseeing Iowa Stars operations, went to work to revive the Black Hawks.

The effort brought back a number of ex-Hawks. Coyle, Swick, John Lesyshen, and many others never really left the community. Jack Barzee, Paul Johnson, Jim Smith, and players who had continued to skate brought their equipment back to Waterloo. The reborn 1970/71 Black Hawks finished second in the USHL. They would win three league titles during the 1970s.

Prior to the Iowa Stars' single season, North Stars President Walter Bush said, "The caliber of people with whom we have dealt in this area was one of the overriding factors that brought us to Waterloo. We think a great deal of the energies and abilities of these men who worked so long and hard to bring the Stars into existence. It would come as no surprise to me if they help make this region into hockey's answer to Green Bay."

Although Bush's remark was not borne out with the Stars, the comparison fits to some degree with the Black Hawks. A mythically successful past, followed by decades with a struggling franchise, and eventually, a brilliant resurgence could describe the timeline for Green Bay Packers or Waterloo Black Hawks history. Although the numbers are much different, the passion of fans for the Black Hawks and Packers is unquestioned, right down to the tailgating. Minnesota executives were even correct about hockey spreading beyond the Cedar Valley to much of Northern Iowa, just not patient enough to enjoy the benefits.

Although there must have been many people disappointed when professional hockey didn't stick in Waterloo, the end result has certainly been a blessing for many young players, coaches, and generations of Black Hawks fans.

Leaving the Old Barn

This article commemorated the 30th anniversary of the final game at McElroy Auditorium. It was posted to waterlooblackhawks.com on December 9, 2024.

Ben Stadey saw all the signs that junior hockey was going to make it in Waterloo. As a 16-year-old rookie defenseman in early 1992, Stadey was there when the United States Hockey League's biggest stars – Chris and Peter Ferraro – were traded to the Black Hawks.

"The Ferraros were so dynamic, and you could see this was where hockey was going," Stadey remembers. "And I thought they were just an amazing combination of skill, talent, and violence."

The twin Ferraros helped Waterloo battle into the 1992 playoffs before moving on to Maine and later the NHL. Meanwhile the Black Hawks and Stadey welcomed young Jason Blake to the Cedar Valley in the fall of 1992. Blake was good that year and spectacular the next, producing a 100-point season in 1993/94 from an even 50 goals and 50 assists. As Blake climbed to the NCAA, Stadey remained for a fourth year in Waterloo, and witnessed the most significant omen of hockey's long-term resurgence in the community.

After 31 seasons at McElroy Auditorium, the Hawks planned to open one more campaign on the National Cattle Congress campus before finishing 1994/95 at Young Arena, still under construction two miles away.

"A lot of us cut our teeth at McElroy, and that's all we knew. I think it's one of those things where you don't know what you have until it's gone," Stadey reflects, now nearly 30 years since the final game at Waterloo's original rink on December 9, 1994.

"It was a great building," says then-Hawks General Manager Scott Brand. "You know it obviously didn't have the amenities that Young has, and it had poles everywhere, but…the thing I remember seeing was a lot of older fans with newer fans. It was kind of like generational to see the fans that had been there in the 60s bringing their grandkids and their kids and saying 'we're leaving home and we're moving to a new home.'"

In 1962, McElroy – also historically called Waterloo Auditorium and the Cattle Congress Hippodrome at different points during its existence – received a major overhaul. The addition of ice-making infrastructure brought the Black Hawks and USHL hockey that fall. The Hawks proved to be the team of the 60s, winning five straight league titles beginning in the spring of 1964. A rink packed with 5,000 people became the expectation on Saturdays and Sundays. In 1969, the Minnesota North Stars moved their top farm club to McElroy, and dozens of future NHL standouts passed through the building during the lone season the Iowa Stars patrolled the rink.

The game and the business of hockey changed in the 1970s. Waterloo was back in the USHL, and the Hawks were generally still competitive, but greater professional opportunities meant more competition for talented players. By the end of the decade, the USHL merged with the Midwest Junior Hockey League, with the intent to convert to all-junior rosters. The championships Waterloo won during the transitional 1977/78 and 78/79 seasons would be the last ever celebrated at McElroy.

The 1979/80 hockey schedule was nearly the last in Waterloo hockey history. Attendance sagged, and the team moved out of town, although another club was acquired and quickly branded the "New" Hawks in the summer of 1980. In large part, the decade which followed resembled a guerrilla campaign to keep hockey alive. If the Black Hawks continued to play, that assured ice would be installed at McElroy, meaning the continuation of youth and high school hockey programs. For many parents, that was better motivation to help the Hawks than any hope junior hockey might find a substantial audience.

The calculus changed in 1993. Across the Cedar River, the Waterloo Diamonds baseball team left town. Waterloo was without pro baseball for the first time in 90 years. With the pipes under McElroy's concrete floor corroding and the building becoming ever harder to maintain, it was increasingly evident that hockey might disappear too. The regret over not building a new ballpark still stung city leaders as they decided the time was right for a new rink.

Even late in its life as a hockey venue, McElroy Auditorium had character. A new ownership group took over in 1992, hiring Brand after his colorful career as a referee. Brand's creativity and promotional flair, plus the arrival of some exceptional players, helped to bring fans back for Black Hawks hockey.

"When that place was sold out, like when we had it going pretty good those two years, it was a really hostile environment," notes forward Rich Metro, who joined the Hawks in 1993. "You could tell you had a home ice advantage, that's for sure."

Uninitiated visiting players had to adjust to some of the building's idiosyncrasies even before stepping on the ice.

"The locker rooms were side by side," says Metro. "The Zamboni doors were behind the net…and that was also the way you went to and from the rink's ice surface. They had metal fold-out chairs and there was an orange carpet that you walked on to go to your locker room. Our locker room was to the left and the visiting locker room was to the right, and basically both were across from each other. So if you got into a fight and got kicked out of the game, you and the guy you fought were literally right next to each other going off the ice."

"It was an old barn and it had a lot of character," says defenseman Wes Blevins, who arrived for the 1994/95 season with the move to Young Arena imminent. "It was tough; the games were physical. The crowds were loud…It was an old, old barn, and it was dark, too. I remember that the lighting was darker, much darker, than Young Arena, that's for sure."

Adding to the home ice edge, Waterloo players like Blevins and Stadey knew how to find their way around McElroy's unique dimensions in that relative darkness.

"McElroy was shaped like an egg," says Stadey. "It was unique. As a defenseman breaking the puck out from the space behind the net – and how oddly narrow the corners were – you really had to adjust your game to that rink."

Not all of McElroy's quirks could be regarded as "advantages."

"People forget that we came in on the tail end of a rodeo every year at the National Cattle Congress," reflects Brand. "For the month of October, it was dead flies everywhere. On the ice. Dead flies all over. I mean, it still smelled like, you know, cow droppings. There was still the dirt they'd used. The seats were still covered in dust."

"It was literally built for the rodeo, right?" Metro notes rhetorically as he also reflects on the locker rooms. "Everyone's stall had a mirror with light bulbs that wrapped around, I think so the rodeo clowns could put their makeup on.

"Sometimes we'd break a pane of glass around the rink, and we had [to replace it with] plywood in the corner. We used to tease Scotty Brand and say that he was selling those seats for half price behind that plywood."

Brand and Head Coach Scott Mikesch had other unique challenges as the 1994/95 season began. Which players would be right for the roster as the team transitioned from the small, asymmetrical ice surface at the Cattle Congress grounds to the big new rink on Commercial Street?

"One of the things we actually asked for is: 'hey, can we just take the same size ice surface from McElroy and move it over?'" says Brand, laughing. "But you know, I think that was the first thing: do you build your team for the first half or the second half?"

One thing was certain: many of the players would come from Michigan. At the time, prospects were often acquired through AAA feeder programs tied to a designated USHL club. Waterloo's connections were in Michigan. In addition, Mikesch himself was from the Upper Peninsula. Metro, Blevins, and a host of others came from the state. So did veterans Bobby Hayes, Todd Steinmetz, Jeff Kozakowski, and Austin Crawford, all members of the 1993/94 Hawks squad which went 33-15-2, enjoying more success than any Waterloo team in more than a decade.

Forward Roger Trudeau was another Michigander. The first-year forward remembers a roster in flux during 1994/95 as the Hawks struggled at the outset.

"We had a lot of people coming in and out of our team that year and had some injuries. We had a lot of players getting traded," says Trudeau, who himself missed much of the early schedule due to knee surgery.

"We had quite the team the year before. We had a lot of guys move on, and it was definitely a rebuilding year," agrees Stadey.

The Hawks did not put together consecutive wins at any time during the first two months of the schedule. Overtimes were especially problematic. Waterloo lost four of them during that early span, including three at McElroy Auditorium. By the time the rink finale arrived on December 9th, the Hawks had just five wins in their first 19 games and had gone winless in five straight.

Brand and the Hawks had played up the farewell campaign for McElroy, and the building saw above average crowds in October and November.

"Not very many teams get an opportunity to do it," says Brand. "You don't know when the last game is [at the end of a season] because of playoffs and stuff like that. So it was a great marketing opportunity."

Unfortunately, hopes for drawing one more 5,000-fan crowd were overly optimistic.

"We were kind of expecting there to be more people," notes Trudeau. "I can't remember for sure, [but] it was a decent crowd."

Official attendance was reported as 3,650.

The Hawks went shorthanded early, and the visiting Thunder Bay Flyers capitalized on the first power play. David Hoogsteen scored the first goal of the night just 5:36 after the initial faceoff. It was a feisty first period, with three sets of offsetting penalties. Waterloo had just finished an unsuccessful power play a minute-and-a-half before Trudeau tied the game, putting a shot under the crossbar to finish a three-on-two rush.

Early in the second, Trudeau gave Waterloo the lead with his second goal. He buried a rebound chance to put the Hawks in front for nearly half of the period. Hoogsteen tied it for Thunder Bay, but Hayes followed up an initial shot to make it 3-2 at 13:03. Waterloo couldn't nurse the lead to intermission. Jason Kelly leveled the score 2:40 before the break.

The third period was scoreless, but the Flyers dominated the overtime. Hawks goalie Jeff Melnechuk made eight saves in just over six minutes of extra play. Thunder Bay's ninth shot won it. Jayme Adduono – who would become a Black Hawk the following season – scored the game-winner at 6:40. The 4-3 result was Waterloo's fifth overtime loss.

Players went down the tunnel and over the orange carpet to their respective locker rooms. The Flyers turned to the right and celebrated. The Black Hawks went left and wondered how another close game slipped away, leaving them with just five wins in their first 20 games.

The Black Hawks announced that McElroy Auditorium itself was the night's #1 star. Fans filed out of the rink one last time. If they glanced back toward the ice surface, they might have seen Brand walk out onto the rink with an empty cup in his hand. Waterloo's general manager scooped up a cup of snow that been chopped up during overtime.

That cup of shavings would go along with the team to Young Arena and provide a symbolic connection between the Black Hawks' new home and the rink where Waterloo players had won, lost, fought, and bled for 32 years.

"Holy Cow. The Circus is in Town"

A follow-up feature about Young Arena's first game appeared on January 14, 2025.

The Black Hawks spent a few extra minutes at McElroy Auditorium.

Their overtime loss on December 9, 1994, ended the team's tenure in the historic building after 32 years. For the next month, Waterloo was on the road. The series of trips started in Rochester just 24 hours later. The Hawks rolled on to games in Thunder Bay during the final weekend before the USHL's holiday break. After Christmas, they were scheduled for four straight away games through early January.

With the team out of town, General Manager Scott Brand returned to McElroy's quiet darkness. As he walked through the deserted locker room, he wondered whether moving downtown would truly be the right thing for Waterloo hockey.

"I remember thinking about all the people that had been there in that locker room, and it was kind of emotional. It was kind of like, 'Geez, it's never going to be [the same],'" Brand says. "I remember leaving there and thinking, 'I don't know about this new rink. What's this going to be like?'"

Brand's uncertainties about Young Arena may have been heightened, because construction had seemed slow throughout the fall. Work was still in progress at the Commercial Street site as players scattered for a 13-day holiday layoff.

"As it was going up, we worried about whether they were going to hit the completion date," Brand remembers. "And actually, they came very close."

Some finishing touches were still missing when the Hawks hosted the Dubuque Fighting Saints on January 14th. Nonetheless, the game which the community had been anticipating for nearly two years was played on schedule. Waterloo players had varying degrees of awareness about the state of the new rink.

"The funny thing is we never really went down to that area very often," remembers forward Rich Metro, who was then spending his second season in the Cedar Valley. "So none of us were really too aware of how it was going – or not going – but they just kept talking about it. So you just never knew when it was going to actually be done."

Defenseman Wes Blevins remembers the anticipation for Young Arena differently. Like Metro, Blevins was from Michigan, but 1994/95 was his first season with the Hawks. The promise of a new rink had been part of what attracted him to Waterloo.

"[Head Coach] Scott Mikesch mentioned that we'd be playing in McElroy for half the season, and then in January once the New Year came, that we'd be moving to our new facility with an Olympic-sized sheet of ice. So yeah, it was definitely brought to our attention before we signed," says Blevins.

"I remember the construction of it and everything," Blevins adds. "I remember walking on dirt before any of the glass was put in or any of that. It was a really nice facility."

Forward Roger Trudeau – yet another Michigander – was also playing his first year of USHL hockey. He returned from an injury in time to be part of the final games at McElroy, and for the road trip which followed.

Trudeau remembers, "We periodically went in and checked it out and saw the progress, but we came back [from Christmas] and BAM: we're in a brand-new rink, and it almost felt like a completely new season.

"For some reason, the smell of the concrete is the first thing that comes to mind; just the new smell of it, but [it was] just total euphoria...That's probably the best way that I could say it. Obviously it's exciting, because you know that every day, you're coming into this beautiful arena...and you really appreciate it a lot."

The building was formally opened to the public during the final days of December, more than two weeks before the first scheduled game in mid-January. During the festivities, the Young family was recognized for contributing the property, in addition to significant financial support for construction. Mayor John Rooff spoke to the large crowd. Cedar Valley figure skaters and youth hockey players had their first opportunity to cut the ice. Toward the end of the evening, everyone on hand was invited to take part in a free public skate, but there were far more people in attendance than the skate rental counter could accommodate.

For Brand and the Black Hawks' staff, the early showing was a chance to talk with season ticket holders about the location of their new seats. Hawks players went to their new locker room stalls before strapping on helmets and stepping out of the tunnel for a scrimmage in front of the sizable audience.

From that evening onward, Waterloo players understood that skating in the new building with Olympic dimensions would be much different than defending the quirky, asymmetrical ice sheet at McElroy Auditorium.

Veteran defenseman Ben Stadey had spent three-and-a-half years patrolling the old rink.

"You had to be a skater [at Young Arena]. If you were not a good skater, maybe you could hide that a little bit better on a small surface," Stadey explains. "The biggest adjustment was just going 'Wow, look at all this room behind the net.' You've really got to change up your game. There's a lot of open ice out here and…you really had to watch it if you were playing man-on-man, because if you got burned…there's a lot more ice that you would have to cover."

Brand says Waterloo and Young Arena were early adopters of an anticipated trend which never materialized.

"At the time, everybody was supposed to go to Olympic ice, and I think we're the only ones now, right?" Brand notes, thinking back on early impressions of the change. "The first time they got to skate on the ice, particularly the defensemen, kind of stopped short of the boards because they were waiting for the [wall to] wrap around. It's like, 'Oh [crap], I've got to take three extra strides to get to the boards,' so I remember the first practice. They're like, 'It's huge!' Everybody was in awe. Just the newness and everything else. But it did take adjusting."

Sometimes the puck went to unexpected places when it bounced off the end wall. Sometimes shots created odd rebounds. It took time to understand the liveliness of the glass and boards. Those things bedeviled defensemen and goalies for a while, but forwards like Metro gladly embraced many of Young Arena's advantages, with one exception.

"It made Scott Mikesch's bag skates even longer," Metro says, half-jokingly.

"At McElroy Auditorium, I think there was only two feet behind the net. It was a really, really small area behind the net, and then you're going into the new arena and you had tons of room…more room to make plays behind the net. You had a little bit more room taking the defenseman wide, attacking with speed. Your entries into the zone were just a little bit different. Teams weren't used to playing on Olympic-sized ice. It's about three or four more hard strides to get the puck."

Right back to the road after taking part in Young Arena's ceremonial opening, the Black Hawks were on the wrong end of a 6-2 decision against the Omaha Lancers December 30th. The next night – New Year's Eve – they were still on the bus as 1994 ended, rolling home from a 4-2 loss against the Sioux City Musketeers. The defeat left the Hawks winless in 11 consecutive games. Although that skid ended with a 6-3 victory over the Madison Capitols the following weekend, Waterloo had earned just six wins from their 27 games. The Hawks' 18 points ranked ninth in the 10-

team USHL on the eve of Young Arena's first game.

Whatever was destined to happen on the ice January 14th, Brand was determined to have Waterloo's staff well-prepared.

"We practiced," Brand recalls. "The week before, we ran through everything with the PA and the lights and everything else. We weren't going to mess this up, because the last thing I wanted to be remembered [for was], 'Hey, it was opening night in Young Arena, and we didn't have any pucks.' So we practiced two or three times."

Even so, during the final days before the long-awaited matchup with the Dubuque Fighting Saints, it became clear that the bleachers behind the west goal would not be installed in time. Four sections beside the Zamboni tunnel would be nothing but concrete steps, 15 rows high. The Hawks advised several hundred fans to bring their own seating for Sections I, J, K, and L.

"In hindsight, it was probably a good thing, because we put more people in the building," Brand reflects.

Dubuque was Waterloo's most significant rival of the era. The Fighting Saints had originated in 1980 when a Black Hawks team was relocated to the Five Flags Center. While Waterloo reorganized in time for the 1980/81 season, the Hawks flailed and the Fighting Saints flourished during much of the decade. By the 1990s, the teams were more evenly matched, and the rivalry still simmered.

"I think that particular year, our team and Dubuque weren't great. We were more towards the bottom of the of the rankings," concedes Trudeau, who also remembers his introduction to the rivalry several months earlier.

"My first time driving to Waterloo from Michigan, I got pulled over for a speeding ticket. It was right in between Waterloo and Dubuque. When the police officer came, I thought maybe I'd try to use that I was going to play for the Waterloo Black Hawks, and maybe it would help me out. He didn't say anything, and he came back with the ticket, and as he left, he goes, 'I'm a Dubuque fan.' I had a 50-50 chance on that one, but it didn't help me out."

In October, the Hawks had scrambled to a 4-4 tie against the Fighting Saints. Dubuque had won both matchups in the months since, including a 3-2 overtime decision during Waterloo's 11-game winless streak. The Fighting Saints walked into Young Arena's visiting locker room for the first time with a 16-10-2 record. They were tied for fifth in the USHL.

"It was a little nerve-racking, because I knew we were outgunned or outmanned, talent-wise, skill-wise," says Stadey. "And you're thinking just, could we maybe not worry about the win, but really 'We've got to play well and represent, and it just can't be a blowout.'"

While players stretched, taped sticks, and adjusted their routines to new surroundings, Brand approached his finish line.

"I just remember looking out the glass windows and seeing the cars and the people lined up two or three hours early," Brand says. "And I was like, 'Holy cow. The circus is in town' and it was just amazing."

The big crowd was officially listed as 3,250. Brand is sure it was unofficially more. They were already lively as the players warmed up. After the pregame skate, Brand ceremonially poured out a cup of water which had been McElroy Auditorium ice, symbolizing the transition from – and connection between – Waterloo's rinks. From there, he climbed to the press counter to join the KWWL television crew broadcasting the game live throughout Northeast Iowa.

"I think everybody was pretty amped up," says Metro. "It seemed like it was a pretty rough game, but it seemed like the crowd was really into it, and there was just a lot of energy built up to that game."

"It was loud," remembers Blevins, who was one of the starters on the ice for the opening faceoff. "It was an electric atmosphere. And you could tell that the fans were really excited to watch us play in our new facility."

Waterloo was turned away on an early power play, giving the Fighting Saints' Andy Powers the chance to score the first goal in the building during a Dubuque advantage midway through the period. It was 2-0 by intermission, and the teams had combined for 36 penalty minutes, including a 10-minute misconduct on Stadey.

"Someone took some liberties. I think I took some liberties back in front of the net with my stick," Stadey explains. "I was a very small defenseman for that era, and I just felt like sometimes you had to carve out your own space, literally and figuratively."

One of his first shifts back on the ice, Stadey helped create the play which sounded Young Arena's goal horn for the first time. He and Metro assisted on Andrew Tortorella's pointblank power play goal.

Dubuque was ahead 3-1 after 40 minutes, but Trudeau and Todd Steinmetz assisted on Eric Brown's goal in the first minute of the third period. The building really roared to life when Brown scored again at 5:30, tying the game through the middle stages of the third.

However, a former Hawks standout contributed to Waterloo's undoing. Defenseman Jeff Kozakowski had recorded 43 points to rank fourth in team scoring a year earlier. He started 1994/95 as a Black Hawk but was among the various players traded as Waterloo struggled through the first half of the schedule. In fact, Kozakowski's departure was sealed when he was on the ice for a Dubuque overtime-winning goal against the Hawks in November. The meeting at Young Arena was the first time the teams had faced each other since that game and the Kozakowski trade which followed.

"When I first got there, he was my defense partner," Blevins notes. "He's two years older than me, but I knew him from Garden City [Michigan]. I learned a lot from him for sure."

With 6:42 to go, Kozakowski assisted on Dan Stepanek's go-ahead goal. It turned out to be the game-winner. The Fighting Saints won 5-3. Although the Hawks had rallied to tie the score in the third, Dubuque outshot the home team 47-18.

A week later, Waterloo earned a home win at Young Arena against the North Iowa Huskies. The team slowly adjusted to their new home ice during the final two months of the regular season. Late-season success at Young Arena kept the Hawks in playoff contention. Waterloo went 6-2-1 during their final nine home games, but a road loss to the Fighting Saints with just over a week remaining ended the Hawks' postseason hopes.

The 1994/95 Hawks had closed one building and opened another. Thirty years ago, they were on hand at a pivot point in Waterloo hockey history. For many, it was also an impactful time for themselves.

"It was one of the best times of my life," notes Blevins. "I went on to play college hockey and then I played in the East Coast Hockey League and pro hockey for almost eight years. But playing in the USHL, playing in Waterloo, definitely prepared me for the next level."

"It was an incredible place to play," says Trudeau. "I have really good memories of playing in Waterloo…My second year, the All-Star Game was there. It was a chance for other players to say 'Oh man, this is a place that I want to play.' You know, it's a lot easier to recruit with a brand-new building, and it was absolutely gorgeous."

"Obviously Waterloo has an unbelievable fan base and such great people that support that program," Metro reflects. "Just for their experience, moving into a new rink had to be extra special, just for the sight lines and being on top of the teams playing. You probably felt a little more a part of it. So I think for them it was well-deserved."

"Waterloo will always have a place in my heart," says Stadey. "I think every player who has played there will say the same thing. I just feel so fortunate…I'd never seen Waterloo until I flew in to live there and play there, and I couldn't have asked for a better town, a better place to live away from home."

For three decades now, Waterloo hockey has been better for having a well-loved, boisterous, Olympic-sized home on Commercial Street.

Old Rivalry to Return

The USHL announced a new Dubuque Fighting Saints team on November 19, 2009; this story appeared on waterlooblackhawks.com.

With an announcement today that Dubuque will return to the United States Hockey League next season, one of the USHL's oldest and fiercest rivalries will be renewed.

From 1980 to 2001, the Waterloo Black Hawks battled the Dubuque Fighting Saints. The founding of the original Dubuque team almost brought organized hockey to an end in Waterloo after two decades in the old USHL senior league. With lagging attendance at McElroy Auditorium in the 1979/80 season, Owner/Coach Jack Barzee moved the Black Hawks to the new Five Flags Center and renamed the club. In turn, hockey fans in Waterloo organized an effort to bring the Hennepin Nordiques from the Twin Cities to Northeast Iowa. Adding fertilizer to the freshly sown seeds of a great rivalry, Hennepin had defeated Waterloo for the Clark Cup in March of 1980.

"When I started in the league in 1984, Waterloo fans where still angry about the original Waterloo hockey team moving to Dubuque a couple years before," said USHL Director of Officiating Scott Brand, who later worked in the front office for both franchises in the 1990s. "Black Hawk fans had seen Dubuque win the league, and I think a couple national championships, while the Hawks struggled. Every game was battle; as a referee you knew you were going to be in for a long night."

Dubuque would dominate the early meetings. The reborn Black Hawks were swept during all eight regular season matchups in 1980/81, then were knocked out of the round-robin playoffs with an 8-7 loss to the Fighting Saints in late March. The Hawks eventually earned their first win against Dubuque on January 9, 1982, a 6-5 overtime decision which saw several Waterloo fans arrested after the game for a near-brawl with Barzee and his players.

Dubuque eliminated Waterloo from the postseason again in 1983 and 1985, with the Hawks surprising the Saints in a five-game 1987 series. The rivalry turned dramatically in Waterloo's favor in January of 1992. Twin brothers Chris and Peter Ferraro were traded from the Fighting Saints to the Black Hawks.

"We went over to the World Junior Championships over in Germany and were very successful personally, my brother and I, as well as the team, and shortly after that, we were traded to Waterloo," said Chris Ferraro. "It was an emotional time, because the year before we had a fantastic year with Dubuque, but we were very comfortable going to Waterloo, because we knew Rob Grillo and our linemate Dean Grillo. We were very good friends with them, and we knew we were going into good hands there."

Chris Ferraro was the USHL's reigning scoring champ when he was traded. Peter Ferraro would lead the league in 1991/92. The summer after the trade, both were drafted by the New York Rangers, and both would eventually reach the NHL. But a game shortly after the swap pitted the Black Hawks against the Fighting Saints in Waterloo.

"It was one of those games where it looked like both teams just wanted to get through the game," remembered Ferraro, "We still respected our teammates from Dubuque. It was more of a coach-player situation which wasn't right."

The Black Hawks took a big lead in the first period, eventually stretching the final score to 16-8. The Ferraro brothers combined for 16 points. With the high score and emotion of the evening, the game took a nasty turn with both coaches involved in an altercation coming off the ice.

The next big game between the Black Hawks and Fighting Saints came almost exactly three years later to the day, when Waterloo got to see USHL hockey for the first time in Young Arena on January 14, 1995. Dubuque took the win 5-3. It was the first of many sell-out crowds in the new building on Commercial Street. The game even drew KWWL's television cameras and was broadcast live throughout northeast Iowa.

Throughout the latter 1990s, both teams struggled to put together winning seasons. From 1995/96 to 2000/01, either the Hawks, the Saints, or both were among the bottom two teams in the USHL standings. Brand says the Black Hawks' deep roots in Waterloo helped them survive the dry years.

"The fans really never gave up on their Hawks. Black Hawk hockey is ingrained into the very fiber of the city; everyone has been to a Black Hawk game. The Waterloo Black Hawks represent Waterloo, a hard-nosed, aggressive – yet honest – team, like the guy who puts the bolt on the John Deere tractor.

"When Five Flags Civic Center was built in Dubuque and the former Black Hawks moved, they won right away. Jack Barzee's team won and played hard, but I think – in my opinion – the fans and the team took winning for granted. Jack was the face of that team, people trusted him, but when he left, they started losing. You can't win every season, and marketing people know, you have to market the event."

After the 2000/01 season, the Fighting Saints moved to Tulsa. After a last place finish the following year, the franchise withered completely. Brand says a new USHL team in Dubuque would benefit from a new building, matched with committed ownership and a front office that could make games entertaining, win or lose.

So after a decade off, can Waterloo and Dubuque raise another epic rivalry?

"Making Dubuque work in the USHL is going to be a lot of hard work," Brand concludes, "but yes, it could be a very viable USHL Market."

Welcome back, old foes.

New Team Churns Up Old Memories

This follow-up article on the return of the Fighting Saints was prepared for publication later in the winter of 2009/10.

The United States Hockey League's return to Dubuque next fall promises to revive a bitter rivalry in northeast Iowa. During the summer of 1980, Waterloo lost its hockey team. Twenty-one years later, the same thing happened in Dubuque.

A couple of decades apart, both cities watched their franchise move to a new home within the USHL. The Dubuque Fighting Saints relocated to Tulsa, took a new name (the "Crude"), finished with the league's worst record in 2001/02, and disbanded permanently at the end of the season. The Waterloo Black Hawks rolled down Highway 20 prior to the 1980/81 campaign, became the Fighting Saints, won the USHL's regular season and playoff championships at the end of the year, and earned undying enmity from their former fans in the Cedar Valley.

"We all really enjoyed playing in Waterloo and it came as a shock when word came out in the spring we were moving to Dubuque," said former Black Hawk and Fighting Saint forward Bob Motzko.

Motzko is now the head coach at St. Cloud State University. He recalls that there was a rivalry between the Fighting Saints and Black Hawks even before the Waterloo franchise was reborn just in time for 1980/81.

"The old history in this story is: that same summer the Hennepin [Minnesota] Nordiques are the team that moved to Waterloo, and we had some history with those returning players."

Hennepin had beaten Waterloo for the Clark Cup, the USHL's playoff trophy, the previous spring during a contentious series. There weren't any punches pulled when Waterloo and Dubuque met for the first time at the Five Flags Center on October 19, 1980; Motzko scored four goals, and the Fighting Saints blew out the Black Hawks 11-4. A month later, the first game played between the teams in Waterloo was even more lopsided, as the visiting Saints scored ten seconds after the opening faceoff and took home a 17-3 win.

Dubuque won every meeting between the clubs in 1980/81. When the Hawks finally found a way to win a game in the series – 6-5 in overtime on January 9, 1982 – it nearly touched off a brawl between Black Hawks fans and the Dubuque team. It wasn't the only time in the ensuing years that a Hawks-Saints game would end with arrests in the stands and even on the ice.

In spite of the extracurriculars, both Dubuque and Waterloo helped to develop some great amateur hockey players. The Fighting Saints can claim Gary Suter, who went on to win the Stanley Cup with the Calgary Flames and eventually appeared in over 1,100 NHL games. Tim Breslin starred for Dubuque a few seasons later, before helping Lake Superior State to a National Championship and four consecutive NCAA tournament appearances. The Black Hawks helped Tom Bissett find his way to Michigan Tech, then briefly the Detroit Red Wings, before a long professional career in Europe. Rod Taylor set most of Waterloo's scoring records and was inducted into the East Coast Hockey League Hall of Fame last winter after spending more than a decade in professional hockey, following his junior and college career.

Two players both teams can claim among their most illustrious alumni are twin brothers Peter and Chris Ferraro. Both reached the NHL and were each still playing minor league hockey until last spring. The pair finished first and second in league scoring during 1991/92, but were traded from Dubuque to Waterloo in January of that season. In a game between the teams just days after the swap, both brothers had a big night during a 16-8 Black Hawk win. The Ferraros combined for 16 points, including a league-record nine for Peter in the single game.

Both franchises found it difficult to win in the late 1990s. After finishing second during the 1993/94 regular season, led by future NHL All-Star Jason Blake, Waterloo would only make it into the top half of the league standings once more before 2002/03. The Fighting Saints finished fifth in 1993/94, then experienced similar struggles before departing for Tulsa.

Bob Mainhardt played in Dubuque in the early 1990s, just before the club's fortunes started to decline. He returned to the USHL this season as the head coach of the expansion Youngstown [Ohio] Phantoms and says he looks forward to seeing hockey in Dubuque's new Mystique Ice Center.

"I've still got friends in the Dubuque area," said Mainhardt, "It always is sad when an organization you played for goes away. The league's going to get stronger; we're going to get a franchise back in a town where we should have one. I'm really excited about it, personally."

And if the new Waterloo-Dubuque rivalry is anything like the old one, hockey fans in both towns should be excited too.

Jack Barzee: Hockey Player

Part I in a Series About Barzee's Remarkable Hockey Journey

This three-part series about Jack Barzee appeared in February of 2021 on waterlooblackhawks.com. In September of that year, Barzee was recognized with the National Hockey League's Lester Patrick Award for outstanding service to hockey in the United States. The award was formally presented in December during U.S. Hockey Hall of Fame ceremonies. This article went live on February 5, 2021.

When Mike Randolph joined the Waterloo Black Hawks as a 19-year-old center in 1971, he had a gold medal-winning U.S. hockey star on his left. Paul Johnson had spurred the 1960 U.S. Olympic team to international hockey's preeminent prize and spent many of the intervening years establishing himself as one of the most talented scorers in the United States Hockey League. In 2001, Johnson was honored with recognition in the United States Hockey Hall of Fame.

On the opposite wing, Randolph found another well-established USHL veteran. Jack Barzee's accomplishments did not draw renown comparable to Johnson, but he had been an effective forward during Waterloo's championship era in the middle 60s. Although he was preparing for his seventh straight season in the league, Barzee was still relatively early in the long hockey life, for which the Black Hawks are now nominating him for the U.S. Hockey Hall of Fame's Class of 2021.

"I had a couple of great linemates," remembered Randolph, the longtime head coach at Duluth East High School. "Jack, on Day One, made me feel comfortable, because I was very young…He just took me under his wing.

"He brought a lot of energy to our locker room, a lot of energy to me as a player. He was very positive on the bench and played the game with a lot of passion. He played the off side – which back then there weren't many players playing the off side – he was a left-handed shot who played the right side."

Randolph's opportunity to play senior hockey in Waterloo came after the Twin Ports native had first moved to Canada to skate at the junior level. Returning to the States and lining up for the Hawks between a pair of veterans, the first-year center was an exceptional addition. Although he may have been the youngest Waterloo player, his older teammates voted him the club's MVP and the United States Hockey League named him Rookie of the Year. Randolph spent the next several years in the professional minor leagues and much of one winter touring with the U.S. National Team. Later transitioning to a behind-the-bench roll, Randolph would begin one of the most successful careers in Minnesota high school history, leading to his induction into the state coaches' association hall of fame in 2018.

"I went on and played in the minors for five more years, and Jack had a lot to do with that, because I saw myself in Jack," Randolph remembers. "Anything around the game, he loved doing, and anybody who hired him would just see that in his personality: that you've got somebody who loves the game and is not doing it as a job, he's doing it as a passion."

A decade before Randolph and Barzee were teammates – when Barzee was roughly the same age as his future center – Barzee's options to pursue his own career were limited.

"When I left high school, if you didn't go to college there were senior teams and minor league hockey, but the American players didn't get the door open very easily," Barzee notes.

He did not take the college route, instead working and playing senior hockey near his home in Connecticut. At age 20 during the winter of 1961/62, Barzee hoped to represent the country on the U.S. National Team. Despite a strong tour with the "Nationals" through January, he was cut with the rest of his line when the squad had the chance to add more experienced forwards. From there Barzee moved from club to club on the senior and minor league circuits, often wearing more than one sweater in the same season: Pittsburgh, Muskegon, Windsor (Nova Scotia), Halifax, among other stops.

"I was a 'bouncin' around' guy for quite a while, and I was getting ready to maybe pack it in when I got a call from Bob Flynn in Waterloo. He was looking for another American player, because they could only list so many Canadians on the roster," says Barzee, who didn't wait long before deciding to come to Iowa.

"The next day I was on the plane with my hockey bag and a couple of suitcases and never looked back."

During the years when Barzee had been hoping to find his way in the sport, Waterloo had shot to the top of the United States Hockey League. The Hawks were .500 in 1962/63, the year they entered the USHL. They went on to scratch out league titles in each of the next two seasons.

Entering the fall of 1965, player/coach Bud McRae and defenseman

Bill Dobbyn provided Waterloo with a formidable blue line. Former Michigan netminder Jim Coyle was well-established in goal. Veteran forwards like Tim Taylor, Duke Dutkowski, and Dave Swick were joined by Johnson during the gold medalist's first full season in the Cedar Valley. With Barzee as part of the group, the Hawks won seven of their first eight league games, on the way to a 21-9-0 record and another closely-contested USHL championship.

"That's the first time I was ever on a winning team in my life," says Barzee, smiling at the memory. "I celebrated maybe for a month…I was just happy to be on the team with those guys. They were all pretty darn good hockey players."

With Barzee contributing in the years which followed, the Hawks were at the top of USHL twice more for a run of five straight titles. The league's team-of-the-decade was most dominant in 1967/68, running away to the USHL crown with a record of 27-6-1.

Barzee did not produce the type of eye-popping offensive totals which Johnson regularly achieved. His play did not lead to National Team opportunities like those which arose for Taylor, Keith Christiansen, and some of his other teammates. However, Barzee was a strong defensive forward and penalty-killer. He also developed a knack for clutch scoring. One of his timeliest goals came during a rare close game with the Hawks at the height of their success in February of 1968. Forcing a Rochester Mustangs turnover with under five minutes to play, he scored unassisted to lift Waterloo to a 2-1 victory amidst a string of 18 wins in 19 matchups.

Hockey income did not provide a viable living for any of the Black Hawks in the 1960s. Like his teammates, Barzee worked outside jobs to continue playing. He primarily paid his bills through summer work as a union elevator technician back in Connecticut, while taking other short-term positions in Waterloo during the season.

"I really didn't want to work; I wanted to just play hockey in the winter. I worked hard enough in the summer," Barzee says, conceding, "I probably would have been a mechanic in the elevator business the rest of my life if I didn't stay in the hockey rink."

When the Black Hawks went dormant for the 1969/70 season to allow the Minnesota North Stars' Central Hockey League affiliate to move into McElroy Auditorium, Barzee stuck with the USHL, joining the Green Bay Bobcats that winter. Minnesota relocated their farm team again the next summer, providing an opening for the Black Hawks to return and for Barzee to move back from Wisconsin. By that time, Waterloo's stable roster of the 1960s had started to shift toward younger players as the sport grew and changed across a wide spectrum.

"When you talk about the players that were in the league in the 60s: the Herb Brooks's and the Lou Nanne's and the George Konik's, there were no other places [for them, because] there were just six teams in the NHL. These guys were good," Barzee notes. "When you got to the 70s, the picture started to change. It was more college kids coming to play in the league and trying to get a job."

The Hawks did not return to championship form, but did finish second during 1970/71 and tied for second in 1971/72. With Barzee advancing into his early 30s, the allure of a new opportunity pulled him away from Waterloo during the 1972 offseason. In fact, it took him out of the country. Barzee moved to the Alps to skate for Kusnacht in the Swiss B League. There he got to know Czech-born player-coach Vladimir Kobranov.

"He was a legend from the Czech National Team in the late 40s…He lived in Zurich and I lived in Kusnacht. He ran the youth program, and I was his assistant with all the young kids, and I learned so much. I was on the ice five hours a day, it was just awesome. I took so much away from that, and I never realized what I had learned until the years started to go by."

Although his time on the ice had nearly run out, when Barzee returned to the Black Hawks for the 1973/74 season, he was still playing at a high level. He averaged a point per game that season (46 of each, with 21 goals and 25 assists). He was also chosen to skate in the USHL All-Star Game just shy of his 33rd birthday. Waterloo ended the year with a stout 29-18-1 record and reached the USHL Commissioner's Cup championship series, falling to the Thunder Bay Twins.

On Thanksgiving in 1973, Barzee produced his most memorable individual performance as a Black Hawk. Waterloo hosted that year's holiday contest against the Milwaukee Admirals, and the adept penalty-killer churned out four points. His two goals and two assists were all shorthanded. The effort contributed to Barzee's career total of nine points on the holiday – a Waterloo hockey fixture to this day – which tie him with Johnson for the most ever on Thanksgiving by a Waterloo skater.

By 1973, the Black Hawks were evolving from a non-profit organization into a business owned by a large number of shareholders in the community. In addition to playing, Jack was the team's publicity director and managed day-to-day operations. His wife, Kathy, worked for the team fulltime, with the couple fully invested in growing the sport.

"I was running around to schools, and selling tickets, and talking up the game and trying to get kids to join the youth program, and talking to the Rotary Club," Barzee remembers of that transitional time.

As he eventually left the ice in the spring of 1975, Barzee's zest for hockey never diminished. The years which followed opened a new phase in his career, during which he was able to create opportunities for a new generation in the sport and a pathway toward advancement that he – and players like Mike Randolph – never had at the same age.

Jack Barzee: Hockey Coach

Part II in a Series About Barzee's Remarkable Hockey Journey

This waterlooblackhawks.com article was posted February 12, 2021.

Bob Motzko was looking for new scenery.

Motzko had been a multisport high school athlete in Austin, Minnesota. By the fall of 1979, the 18-year-old forward had graduated and joined his hometown Austin Mavericks to further refine his hockey skills. After six games, Motzko knew he would benefit from a change of surroundings.

"I wanted to move away from home and have that experience playing junior hockey," remembered the current head coach of the Minnesota Gophers. "I had played in a bantam tournament in Waterloo, Iowa, and [met] Craig Brown. Craig was playing with the Waterloo Black Hawks, Greg Davis was the goalie, and Kevin Landau and Bill Kammeyer were four Waterloo guys I had met. So I told my coach 'I want to go to Waterloo.'

"Jack Barzee probably gave me a week or two try-out, but I ended up playing the whole season...and boy was I fortunate that I had that experience to get to Waterloo."

With the USHL transitioning to all-junior rosters that season, Barzee added the 5-foot, 11-inch right-handed winger, noting at the time that Motzko "has good speed and is smart around the net. He could be more physical, but hustles all the time and is always improving."

Motzko's opportunity to move from Southern Minnesota to the Cedar Valley was possible thanks to an innovative solution Barzee had helped to engineer earlier in the decade while the USHL was fraying under the weight of financial losses.

Barzee had become a Black Hawks executive even before playing his final games for the team in 1975. His role came with various titles but involved all manner of promotion, sales, and organization for the club. Walt Kyle Jr. – then a teenaged player – saw firsthand how far Barzee's responsibilities extended.

"I had a front row seat at our kitchen table most mornings as Jack would come to our house and meet with my father – a CPA by trade and later commissioner of the USHL – and work tirelessly to keep hockey in

Waterloo. I know that if not for Jack, Waterloo would have lost hockey," said Kyle, who would go on to become head coach at Northern Michigan University from 2002 through 2017 among other achievements during a career which continues today as a hockey scout.

"The attendance started to kill us," Barzee recalled. "I don't think the economy was that great at the time."

On the ice, the Hawks were struggling too. A run of five straight championships in the 60s, followed by competitive finishes – including consecutive appearances in the league championship series in 1974 and 1975 – set expectations high. Frustration set in when the 1976/77 Hawks started poorly. Coach Dave Swick, Barzee's friend and former teammate, was suspended by the USHL at Thanksgiving for lashing out at a referee, temporarily putting Barzee on the bench for the first time, on top of his other responsibilities to the team. By January "Head Coach" became a permanent part of his job description too. He helped the team to a 12-8-0 finish, but bigger problems awaited.

"Milwaukee jumped to the International League, and we were sitting there with three teams left in the U.S. League, it was Green Bay, Sioux City, and Waterloo, and the Midwest Junior League was sitting there with St. Paul, Bloomington, and the Austin Mavericks," said Barzee. "We just put our heads together and said 'Well, how can we do this?'

"So we decided that the three old USHL teams would only have 12 older players on the team and if we could, we would use 20- and 21-year-old players that had played junior the year before in the Midwest Junior League."

Kyle would become one of those older players during the 1978/79 season as he transferred from Boston College to Northern Michigan. That season playing for Waterloo provided a bridge as he eventually helped both schools reach the Frozen Four during his NCAA career.

"In my opinion, Jack's greatest legacy will always be the role he played in the late 70's in the merger between the old USHL senior league and the upstart Midwest Junior Hockey League," Kyle said. "If Jack had not been the point-of-the-spear, this merger may have never happened, and today's USHL may never have come to fruition."

A financing agreement arranged by Sioux City owner Gary Lipschutz also put Barzee in a more stable financial situation. The USHL took over nominal ownership of the team from local shareholders by paying off the club's debts. Barzee remained in charge, running all aspects of the organization with assistance almost exclusively from his wife, Kathy.

On the ice, the Hawks found success again as the former USHL clubs surged to the top of the league. Waterloo and Sioux City tied for the

USHL's best regular season record in 1977/78 before the Hawks prevailed during an epic seven-game championship series. The next year, Waterloo swept to both the regular season and playoff titles. Barzee led Waterloo to a 72-39-0 regular season record during those two transitional years.

By 1979, the USHL was confident it could proceed with exclusively junior players. League leaders also officially turned over ownership of the Black Hawks franchise to Barzee, creating both opportunities and challenges.

"I pulled some strings with Walt Kyle Sr. and got a loan from one of the banks," Barzee explained. "I went and borrowed money one day and paid it back two days later, and went and borrowed it the next day and paid it back three days later."

If Barzee was "robbing Peter to pay Paul," as he describes it, Waterloo's performance on the ice didn't suffer in 1979/80. Nor did he suffer from no longer having any older senior players on his roster.

"I was very fortunate to have a lot of hockey contacts," Barzee said demurring credit for building another winner. "People called to say 'Hey, I've got a player.' Everybody used to laugh at my phone bill, but I only spent $2,000 recruiting, and everybody else spent $12-or-$14,000."

Motzko corroborated Barzee's extensive networking: "He went on to many years of success finding hockey players that really wanted to play…he could go to Alaska, he could go to the east coast, he could go to Minnesota. Jack had his contacts and knew where to find players to be successful."

The first all-junior Hawks team won a division title with a 27-19-2 mark and reached the Clark Cup Championship Series. The team's final games together came during USA Hockey's National Junior Tournament in Detroit. After the season was over, Barzee led a team of USHL All-Stars to Switzerland for the Beard Cup tournament. It was the first of three such trips to the country where Barzee had spent one year during his playing career and learned elementary lessons about coaching as he worked with Swiss youth hockey players.

The USHL squads faced opponents from Czechoslovakia, Germany, and Switzerland, finishing second twice and third once.

Back stateside in 1980, the Waterloo hockey community had not adapted well to the disappearance of senior players. The perception of a diminished level of play by junior-aged teams could not be overcome. Barzee had shifted several 79/80 Hawks games to "neutral" ice at the new Five Flags Center in Dubuque. With his prospects in Waterloo apparently diminishing, Barzee relocated his team to Dubuque during the offseason (hockey would survive in Waterloo with the subsequent relocation of the

USHL's Hennepin Nordiques before 1980/81 began).

Speaking to potential partners for the new Dubuque Fighting Saints, Barzee told them, "'We're going to go into this with our hat in our hand. We don't know what's going to happen. I've got five players that played with me in Waterloo...We need to raise $25,000 to get the program started.' I had a game plan and a budget of $105,000, and we were lucky that year."

"We sold out almost every game after the first couple," remembered Motzko. "I know there were a couple of fights that got the crowd going, and it was just probably at the right place at the right time."

Beyond the limited number of Waterloo veterans, Barzee built a winner from a roster of skaters cast off by other clubs.

"Sixteen of the players that were on that team were cut from other junior teams in the league," said Barzee. "They just wanted to win so bad, and they loved playing the game. It was pretty breath-taking when I put them out on the ice. I couldn't wait for that hour-and-a-half practice; it was the best time of the day."

Barzee's charges delivered, winning the regular season Anderson Cup by 19 points, steamrolling through the playoffs to claim the Clark Cup, and finishing with USA Hockey's Gold Cup as the top junior team in the country.

More success would follow as the Fighting Saints and the USHL became an increasingly significant destination for American junior talent, like Gary Suter, who would help Dubuque to another three-cup sweep in the 1982/83 season.

"Not a lot of colleges came in to watch the USHL at that time," said Motzko, "but the reputation grew mightily. Jack was going to build his teams on toughness and talent."

Motzko and others who skated for Barzee in the early 80s credit him for bringing out the most in them.

"As a player, you could feel Jack's energy," shared Doug Claggett by email. Claggett joined the Saints from the Seattle area for two seasons beginning in 1982. "You knew he was your biggest champion and advocate. Because of that, players played for him. And in turn, they became advocates of him and the USHL as well...He attracted great players to the entire USHL. He was instrumental in building the USHL into the league that it is today."

As to coaching style or philosophy, Barzee shared the same enthusiasm for the sport which he had as a player.

"I was never a 'blackboard guy;' I was never an 'x's and o's' coach," he reflected. "I was lucky enough and healthy enough and a good enough skater to have sweats on every day and go out on the ice to demonstrate things…And then, just believe in the player. I tried never to put a player in a situation where he would be embarrassed. I think setting up a player to be successful and making him be a realist and accept his role was probably my best asset."

It proved successful for Dubuque. Over five seasons leading the Fighting Saints, the organization claimed two Anderson Cups, three Clark Cups, and two USA Hockey National Junior titles. Barzee's Dubuque squads skated to an aggregate regular season mark of 156-80-4. Adding in his time with the Hawks coaching senior, junior, and hybrid teams, he was 267-146-6 with three outright regular season championships and five USHL postseason crowns in less than nine full years.

"I was there in its infancy as it started," Motzko summed up. "Jack is one of the true pioneers of junior hockey in the United States and one of the all-time greatest general managers and coaches."

As a pioneer, Barzee would continue to break ground for American players during a new phase in his hockey life, which began in the offseason following Dubuque's third Clark Cup.

Jack Barzee: Hockey Scout

Part III in a Series About Barzee's Remarkable Hockey Journey

This article completed the series on February 19, 2021.

PK O'Handley's first United States Hockey League team did not win a lot of games.

The 1991/92 North Iowa Huskies finished the season 14-33-1. The club avoided a last place finish by just four points, edging out only the Wisconsin Capitols. In the ten-team league, North Iowa was one of two to miss the Clark Cup playoffs. The results fell short of aspirations the 24-year-old head coach had for his team. One night, O'Handley's frustration was evident from the stands as NHL scout – and former United States Hockey League Coach of the Year – Jack Barzee looked on.

Barzee went to O'Handley's office after the game.

"I think he spent as much time evaluating my performance as the players on the ice, and he let me know, and I'll always appreciate that. It's had a large impact on my career," recalled O'Handley, who today is the head coach with the most wins in USHL history. "The guy cares, and he cares about people who care about the game."

O'Handley and Barzee saw each other with regularity throughout the 1990s, with Barzee working for NHL Central Scouting and O'Handley building North Iowa into a winning program as the decade continued. As Barzee spent time gauging prospects as part of Central Scouting's mission to identify talent on behalf of the NHL's teams collectively, O'Handley noted something else about his visits to the North Iowa Fairgrounds and other facilities around the USHL.

"It wasn't just about the potential NHL player. When he was scouting and he would come into a building, it wasn't rare – it wasn't rare for Herb Brooks to do the same – he might say, 'I want to talk to so-and-so on your team' and scold that player a bit. But at the same time, Jack built the player up and tried to make him understand that it's the greatest game in the world, and maybe that player was wasting a little bit of their talent."

"Growing up in the game, and having the opportunities to do what I did in the game, it's the only thing I ever really wanted to do," Barzee said when asked to reflect on the candid observations he offered to prospects, coaches, and lunch pail players alike, "I would see someone hurting or see a coach that I thought was making the wrong decisions...I wouldn't go up and try to tell them I know it all or anything like that. I would just say, 'Hey, I got a couple thoughts I'd like to share with you. I noticed you were doing this and doing this, and have you ever thought of trying this?'

"I always felt I had something to offer, because I loved the game, and I think God gave me a gift, because I could sometimes see the game differently than a lot of other people."

Following the five years he owned and coached the Dubuque Fighting Saints from 1980 to 1985, Barzee was ready to use his hockey insights in a new way. Dubuque had won the Clark Cup playoff trophy three times, two Anderson Cup regular season titles, and two Gold Cup USA Hockey national junior titles. Nonetheless, the daily challenges and stresses of managing all aspects of the Fighting Saints operation were taking a toll. In season, it was routine for Barzee to work 80-hour weeks, with little relief in the summer as he built the next year's squad, sold season tickets, and arranged sponsor partnerships.

By the summer of 1985, Barzee knew it was time for something different. Initially, he hoped to stay in coaching: "There were 11 college coaching jobs open that year, which was amazing. That doesn't happen very often. But it didn't happen for me.

"I was working at a hockey camp up in Nisswa for Minnesota Hockey Camps with Chuck Grillo, and I got a phone call from Jim Gregory of the NHL," Barzee remembered about one of the most important moments during his time in the sport. "There were 300 guys out for the job I got, and he asked me if I would move to Minnesota and come to work for him. The hockey gods were looking after me."

Over the decades, thousands of players' lives changed when Gregory would call their names as moderator of the NHL Draft. Gregory's call to Barzee was similarly life-altering for the then-44-year-old. Freed from the responsibilities of coaching and ownership, Barzee was positioned to watch top players all over North America. As he planned to see as many as 300 games each year, getting there was the only hard part.

"I was on the road three weeks at a time," Barzee explained, outlining a typical trip early in his Central Scouting career. "I would fly to Winnipeg and take a bus to Brandon, Manitoba, with a suitcase, meet a scout from Regina who had a car. We'd watch the game, and then we'd drive all the way back to Regina, and it was like that until I would end up three weeks later in Portland, Oregon. And this is February in the snow, it wasn't a rose garden. It was in and out of the hotels and eating and having a few beers, then travelling the next day to a game."

While the travel was tough, the hockey was often amazing. Barzee saw a generation of players during his early Central Scouting years – and a four-season sojourn with the Washington Capitals – who themselves have gone into the Hockey Hall of Fame and U.S. Hockey Hall of Fame during the first decades of this century.

Joe Sakic with Swift Current and Mike Modano of Prince Albert in the Western Hockey League.

Jeremy Roenick and Tony Amonte in prep school at Thayer Academy.

Keith Tkachuk in Massachusetts and Brian Leech in Connecticut.

Based in the Twin Cities but traveling from one side of the continent to the other, Barzee could see American players making gains as the hockey world was getting bigger. In high school, prep school, midgets, and juniors there were skaters worth seeing. Still, longstanding beliefs among hockey executives were challenging to sway.

"I used to say, 'Hey you guys, don't knock this kid that's playing high school hockey in Hibbing, Minnesota. He's going to be right next to that guy right there that you're talking about who's playing [juniors] in Calgary' and the next thing you know, three years later, those two guys are playing on the same line and you couldn't tell the difference," Barzee said.

"If a player belonged 12th overall [on the Central Scouting] ranking list but he was playing high school or college hockey in those days when I first started, then he had to be put somewhere like 40th in the first ranking, and he had to keep proving himself and gradually they'd move him up. There was a bias, but I learned to live with it. I knew it was a fight, and I came prepared."

Barzee's former Waterloo Black Hawks teammate and Duluth East High School Coach Mike Randolph had seen the same enthusiasm in Barzee's personality when they had been linemates in Waterloo during the 1970s, and noted, "Jack is all for the American hockey player – was all for the American hockey player back then – and it was a tough sell, so American hockey was very fortunate to have a person like Jack in the position that he was."

Former Waterloo and Dubuque player Bob Motzko – now the head coach of the Minnesota Gophers – echoed that sentiment, "He stayed very connected and involved and was a believer in the USA system, the USHL system, and the college system. Knowing Jack – and Jack's got a strong personality – he would have fought like heck for the U.S. player at every turn as he was scouting, and I'm sure people at the NHL level leaned on him heavily for expertise."

NHL clubs weren't the only ones to benefit from Barzee's perspective on the game. The 1990s were a disruptive period in the USHL. Many longstanding league members relocated. Others passed to new ownership or moved into new facilities. New and dynamic organizations joined the circuit in previously untapped markets. The arrival of Gino Gasparini as league commissioner in 1995 contributed to a sequence of events which culminated in the USHL becoming the nation's only Tier I league in 2002, providing junior players with a combination of equipment, facilities, coaching, and academic support unsurpassed around the world and now an important component within USA Hockey's American Development Model.

As that long process played out, Barzee was doing more than watching hockey games.

"You look at Gino Gasparini, you look at Herb Brooks, you look at Jack Barzee: they got with a bunch of owners and said what this could be," said O'Handley, "Quite frankly they had a crystal ball that it could be a large feeder for the National Hockey League in times to come, if you took the right steps and invest the right money. You know, as much as Jack was a scout, a coach, an owner, and all those things, he was a heck of a salesman. He – with others – was a driver in setting forth the vision of what this has become."

"I never stopped promoting the league no matter where I was at. I kept very tight with [former USHL Board Chairman] Butch Johnson and Gino and Herbie and a lot of people who were really supportive of the league, and I just kept telling them, 'Don't worry about what everyone else is doing. Just do your own thing.'"

In 2005, the USHL honored Barzee with its Distinguished Service Award, noting at the time that his position with Central Scouting "...allows him to further champion the cause of the players of the USHL."

Today, nearly a decade after Barzee retired from Central Scouting in 2012, the USHL is consistently producing substantial numbers of NHL Draft picks: 51 players in 2020. The gold medal-winning 2021 U.S. National Junior Team included 23 players with ties to the league. USA Hockey's National Team Development Program has found important competition against 13 other USHL clubs this season and each year since 2010/11.

"People listen to him, and his hand prints are all over U.S. hockey," said O'Handley, concluding, "As a player, as a coach, as a manager, as an owner, as a scout, I think he certainly was a builder in what we're seeing today. If there's a guy in American hockey who belongs in the U.S. Hockey Hall of Fame, it's Jack Barzee."

Camping in Carolina

Drury Makes Second Summer Trip

Jack Drury provided fans with a look at his NHL development camp experience in the Preseason 2019 edition of Hawk Tawk Mag-e-Zine.

There aren't many hockey players who wear #72. But at age 19, when there is an NHL logo on the front of the sweater, perhaps you're not as concerned with what's on the back.

Former Waterloo Black Hawk forward Jack Drury has now worn #72 for back-to-back summers during the Carolina Hurricanes' annual Prospects Development Camp. This year's gathering of Carolina draft picks and other young players was held at PNC Arena in Raleigh during the closing days of June.

Drury was well-equipped to make the trip to North Carolina for the second time late last month.

"You're able to prepare for it a little better, because you know what's going to happen," Drury said. "You know what the days are going to look like, so mentally, you're able to get yourself more ready."

Mentally and physically, the camp was a different experience back in 2018, when Drury found himself in new surroundings just days after being selected 42nd overall by the Hurricanes during the second round of the NHL Draft.

"I didn't have much time. I got drafted on Saturday, and we had to report to development camp on Tuesday, so it was a pretty quick turnaround. I flew home Saturday, had one day at home, and packed up my stuff and flew to Carolina."

In 2018, Drury had just finished his second season with Waterloo. He was one of the youngest players on hand as the Hurricanes' prospects gathered in the PNC Arena locker room.

"I sat next to Martin Necas – who played for their AHL team last year – and across the locker room was Andrei Svechnikov [the second overall pick in the 2018 Draft]. Those guys were really in a league of their own," Drury remembered. "They still talked to the younger guys and made us feel like we were part of the same family."

Of course, Drury spent a lot of time with the other Carolina prospects, but the experience was different from many of the other camps he had attended throughout his years of youth and junior hockey.

"The development camps…are incredibly focused on off-ice stuff. I know some teams do a lot of games, but in Carolina we play one three-on-three game at the end, and that's it…[People] think of all-games-and-skating, but at least for Carolina, there's a huge focus on the off-ice element and the conditioning element."

Last summer, work in those areas was simultaneously part of Drury's preparation for the transition to college hockey in 2018/19. Joining the Harvard Crimson in the fall, he was an immediate contributor. During his first NCAA appearance, Drury had three assists in a 7-6 loss to Dartmouth.

Although Harvard was winless after four games, Drury could hardly have had a better beginning to his college career. He recorded points in seven of his first 11 games, and by Christmas break, he had four goals and eight assists. The Crimson took off following the holidays, entering their conference tournament at 17-9-3, before ultimately qualifying for the NCAA tournament. Drury ended the year tied for fourth in team scoring with 24 points (nine goals, 15 assists).

Even as postseason qualifiers, Harvard had wrapped up play by the end of March. Instead of three days to prepare for his second appearance at Carolina Prospects Development Camp, Drury had most of three months. He was also prepared to help the wide-eyed, newly-drafted Hurricanes in the same situation he had faced the previous summer.

"It's a good chance to practice [some] leadership and show the younger guys the way the camp works and try to help out as many guys as possible."

Away from the ice, NHL prospect camps have also recently acquired a reputation for fun team-building experiences, which often find their way onto social media.

"My first year, we went to the Fortnite headquarters, which are in Raleigh," Drury explained. "I don't play Fortnite, so for me, that wasn't a blast, but I think everyone else in the camp had a really fun time doing that. This year, we went go-karting."

Now this week, Drury is moving almost as fast as he would in a go-kart during another significant summer camp. At USA Hockey Arena in Michigan, Drury is trying to make the U.S. National Junior Team roster for the second time and earn a return trip to the World Junior Championships.

"The USA Hockey camp is almost strictly games…to evaluate your talent," Drury explained. "You're all trying to make the same team, so it's a bit more competitive in that aspect, and there are not any workouts or off-ice testing. It's just playing games against the other countries and trying to do the best you can."

During last season's World Junior Tournament, the United States had a thrilling run in British Columbia. Drury and his American teammates won the silver medal last January, marking the fourth consecutive year that Team USA has earned a top-three finish. It's part of a remarkable list of moments (the NHL Draft, the NCAA Tournament, an impressive freshman year at Harvard, and two Hurricanes Prospects Development Camps) in 14 months since Drury played his last game as a Black Hawk.

Not that long ago, his experience trying to earn a place on the Waterloo roster during summertime camps provided a basis for much of what has followed.

"[In] the Waterloo orientation camps and main camps, it's summer, but you've got to bring your "A" game, because you're being evaluated, and I think that trend is taken even farther [now]…when it's the end of June or July but you're still getting evaluated and have got to be on your "A" game."

With such an early start – and balanced between the Hurricanes' emphasis on off-ice training and Team USA's competitive process for selecting the 2020 National Junior Team – expect Drury's "A" game to be better than ever during his sophomore season at Harvard this fall.

Russell Rolls into New Season

COVID-19 affected the hockey experience at all levels. Former Hawk Patrick Russell recorded his observations of returning to action with the Edmonton Oilers in this waterlooblackhawks.com article on January 14, 2021 just as the NHL was about to resume competition.

The "Taxi Squad" is a new designation as this abbreviated National Hockey League season begins. Each NHL club will have up to a half dozen players on hand to fill lineup voids created by injury or illness.

At least three former Waterloo Black Hawks have already been given Taxi Squad assignments. That designation puts both Shane Bowers in Colorado and Dylan Samberg in Winnipeg on the cusp of their NHL debuts.

Meanwhile, Patrick Russell has already skated in regular season contests for the Edmonton Oilers. Although being on the team's Taxi Squad makes him unlikely to be in the lineup as the 56-game schedule opens tonight, Russell is otherwise right where he wants to be since signing his first Oilers contract in 2016.

"The organization has taken great care of me. They've obviously shown that they believe in me; they know what kind of player I am," Russell said recently, adding, "I think personally I've taken steps every year to prove that I can play in this league, so it's a partnership [with Edmonton] that goes hand-in-hand. I didn't want to play anywhere else this season, that's for sure."

Following two full seasons with the Oilers' American Hockey League affiliate in Bakersfield, Russell's first chance to skate in Alberta was during an Edmonton-Calgary rivalry game in November of 2018. He appeared in five more games that year, plus another 45 last winter. As an NHLer, Russell has recorded five assists.

"You're always wanting more…you want to keep taking a step and try to play more games in the NHL, but it's a tough year. We're going to need a lot of guys. We have 17 games in 30 days to start out the season, so it's going to be a lot of rotation, and whatever happens, you've just got to be ready. When you're called upon you've got to show up and perform."

The Black Hawks were Russell's first North American stop on his way to the NHL. In 2013/14, Russell shined for Waterloo, leading the team and ranking fifth in the USHL with 29 goals, included ten power play scores and four game-winners. The Hawks claimed the Anderson Cup, earning a league-high 93 standings points, a team record. Russell advanced from Waterloo to St. Cloud State University. During two seasons with the Huskies, he recorded 63 points in 78 appearances and was a point-per-game player (38 points in 38 games) as a sophomore. In addition to his time in junior, college, and professional hockey, the native of Denmark has also had opportunities with his country's national team.

Yet getting home to Denmark during the recent offseason was challenging in a year of international travel restrictions caused by COVID-19. After flying across the Atlantic, Russell had to quarantine for a week.

"At that point, when we got home, I hadn't seen my family in over a year I think, so it was really nice being home to spend a little bit of time to see friends and family," Russell says.

His return to Edmonton in late 2020 meant another 14 days isolating after the trip.

In addition to Russell, most of the world's best hockey players have made their way to central Alberta in the last six months. Edmonton hosted most of the Stanley Cup playoffs during August and September, then the IIHF World Junior Championships, which ended earlier this month.

"I think the City of Edmonton and the NHL did a great job," Russell says of the long-delayed postseason. As for the World Junior Tournament (Russell had previous experience representing Denmark in that event when he was under 20): "It was exciting to have some hockey back on TV…I watched a lot of games and it was some really good hockey with some great young players in that tournament."

For the moment, Russell will likely still remain a spectator on game days while he is on the Oilers' Taxi Squad. However, he will still be involved in club activities, including practices. That will routinely put him on the ice with some of hockey's most exciting players like Connor McDavid and Leon Draisaitl.

"Watching [McDavid] every day, you're amazed at the small things he does, day-in and day-out. He's probably the first guy on the ice. You just watch and try to learn, even though it's pretty much impossible, because he just has what no one else really has," Russell notes.

When it comes to game situations on the ice with the Edmonton stars, Russell's objective is basic: "Give them the puck. It's pretty simple, just give them the puck and try to be a presence in front of the net; stay out of the way and hopefully you can scramble some pucks in there."

Due to challenges crossing the U.S./Canada border, Edmonton and the

NHL's other six Canadian teams will spend this winter playing in one division stretching from Montreal to Vancouver. That may mean some long trips, but Russell anticipates that fans will embrace the short-term situation.

"It will create a lot of rivalries. We already have a great one with Calgary, obviously. I think we're going to play them ten times this year, so it's a lot of the same teams, there's going to be a lot of emotion out there, especially when you play back-to-back and meet the same players the night after, so it's going to be a lot of fun. It's going to be a lot of battles and a lot of emotion out there."

The first of those battles for the Oilers is tonight against the Vancouver Canucks. The puck drops at 9 p.m. Central Time.

Draft Delayed, Dream Continues

Prospects Work Out, Wait for October

The global pandemic altered the NHL Draft schedule in 2020; Hawks players talked about that in Hawk Tawk Mag-e-Zine*'s September issue.*

Any elite-level hockey player spends his draft year wondering what will happen in June.

Hearing his name announced by a National Hockey League club, seeing it on the board beside the top prospects in his age group, and taking a definite step toward the lifelong goal of pro hockey is an experience never to be forgotten. During 2020, June will be in the distant past before those things happen. The New York Rangers will finally make the first pick of 217 by the league's 31 clubs on October 9th.

And many of the typical rituals won't happen during a draft which will be held online due to COVID-19. Rather than traveling to Montreal, players will be watching their phones, computers, and televisions for the latest updates when picks are announced. That is, if they aren't on the ice for practice during a new season which may already be underway.

During parts of the spring and summer, ice time for practice wasn't available – to draft prospects or anyone else – while facilities closed for the global pandemic.

"The first month or so, everything was shut down so it was tough to find ways to get the best training," notes forward Wyatt Schingoethe. "Luckily, I had access to a gym and a trainer to send me workouts. Now I can go to a gym regularly and skate as well."

In April, Schingoethe was ranked 91st by NHL Central Scouting among North American skaters eligible to be picked this year. He made a big jump to that position after being 132nd in the January midterms. Last season, he produced 38 points (17 goals, 21 assists) in 47 Black Hawks games, finishing third in team scoring.

Meanwhile, Waterloo goalie Gabriel Carriere tied for second in the USHL with 21 victories. That helped him secure the 23rd spot in the draft rankings for North American goalies. Carriere says training space wasn't any easier to find near where he lives in Ottawa.

"I've been working out at home for most of the summer since my gym shut down and only opened back up a couple weeks ago. I have also been able to get back on the ice with my goalie coach a couple times a week."

Now Carriere is on campus at the University of Vermont. Ryder Rolston also has Division I college facilities at his disposal. Rolston scored 16 times and accumulated 33 total points during the Black Hawks' pandemic-shortened season. He will go into next month's draft ranked 102nd by NHLCS.

"Since May, I have been really focusing on getting stronger in the weight room. I have been lucky to have the luxury of easy access to a gym, so I've been taking that really seriously."

Rolston and many other 2020 draft hopefuls missed out on a chance to show their raw strength when the NHL's June Combine was cancelled.

"I particularly was looking forward to the combine, because I feel that I would've been able to show my athletic ability off the ice, as well as meet with teams in person," Rolston says.

Besides tests of strength and conditioning, the combine also serves as a chance for team executives to talk directly with the players they are considering. Technology has allowed those meetings to continue.

"Since March, it's been all video calls with teams, which has been a great experience and a great opportunity to meet the teams, hear their feedback, and go through the interview process," Schingoethe says.

Rolston adds, "Not having the combine, things were a little jumbled in terms of meeting with teams, but Zoom has been a good alternative."

While occasional details about the draft have reached the players in other ways, for the most part they have been following along with the same news sources as everyone else.

"I get most of the updates from social media, or friends and family," says Carriere.

One experience loosely related to the draft which is unlikely to be salvaged in 2020 is being called to an NHL team's prospect camp in the days and weeks after being picked.

"For me, it is disappointing," says Carriere. "I would've loved to participate in one of them, given the opportunity, because it would have been a good opportunity to meet some new people and make connections."

While Rolston and Carriere are meeting new people at every turn during their first semesters at their respective colleges (Carriere preparing for his time with the Catamounts and Rolston at Notre Dame), Schingoethe could become the first Black Hawk to ever be drafted during a USHL season.

"Hopefully some family and friends could come in town and all watch it together."

Wherever they're watching, those friends and family (and Black Hawks fans) will have reason to be proud when the longest draft year ever finally comes to an end.

Bubbling Enthusiasm

Starting a Unique Season in a Unique Way

One additional Hawk Tawk Mag-e-Zine *feature focused on COVID-19 alterations in November 2020.*

By their very nature, bubbles are fragile. They separate what's inside from what's outside with the thinnest of layers. Typically they disappear without a trace. The Black Hawks are hoping their training camp COVID-19 bubble will have longer-lasting impacts.

As players arrived on October 1st, they experienced a series of protocols designed to protect them and the Cedar Valley community. In the middle of a global pandemic which had delayed the beginning of the United States Hockey League season, each player was tested for the virus before they left home and then again immediately after they arrived. Even with results back the next day, players practiced, ate, slept, and spent the rest of their first Waterloo week in group isolation.

"COVID has been really scary," said new Black Hawks forward Max Sasson, adding, "The fact that Waterloo and the staff here is really looking out for us [made me] really excited to see the procedures, and I hope all the other USHL teams are doing the same."

Black Hawks trainer Todd Klein played a prominent role in organizing the camp protocols to bring players back to Young Arena.

"Even while they are in the locker room, they wear masks," Klein said. "The only time they get to take those off is as they're leaving the locker room to go on the ice. When they come back off the ice, their masks go back on."

Temperature checks also became part of the daily routine. The team found ways to put more space between players at the rink. And Young Arena staff diligently cleaned all manner of rink surfaces.

However, the unique part of the Black Hawks' effort was keeping players at The Courtyard by Marriott throughout the week.

"It was different for sure, but I think the way the staff set it up was really good, and the guys did a good job with it," said veteran Wyatt Schingoethe. "We have a goal to play hockey and win. If we keep focusing on that, we'll do a good job with these things throughout the year."

Still, Schingoethe conceded that the Black Hawks' 2020 camp was a unique experience in his hockey career.

"In other camps, you have more time for [formal] team activities, and I think we did a good job with that. We tried to do stuff at the hotel, and it was a lot of fun."

Defenseman Mason Reiners was able to participate in those activities, even though he was off the ice while working his way back from a long-term injury. For Reiners, the camp experience kept him right in the midst of team-building for all but the few hours when his teammates stepped between the boards.

"A lot of the stuff we did was spending time together and getting to know everyone," Reiners described. "One of the main things we did was play cards with each other and stuff like that."

Even with two ice sessions each day, there was still plenty of time for whatever else the players could organize. After practice in the morning and a scrimmage in the afternoon, Sasson said the Hawks found ways to keep busy.

"We'd head back to the hotel, we'd have dinner. Once all our [initial] tests came back negative, we were allowed to go to the commons area. We watched football and basketball, and just hung out as a team. I thought it was really good that we all meshed together."

The Hawks are hopeful that the health procedures put in place during October, and a greater degree of enforced but necessary togetherness, will make this a season which is remembered for more than COVID-19.

A Koopman Combo

Hawk Tawk Mag-e-Zine*'s December 2017 edition sketched the path Matt and Kyle Koopman followed to Waterloo. The twin brothers later attended Providence College together starting in 2018/19.*

When Kyle and Matt Koopman first see each other each day, it's not exactly like looking in a mirror. For one thing, Kyle wears a mustache, which he started to grow at the beginning of November. Meanwhile, Matt has chosen the clean-shaven look since "Mo-vember" came to an end.

The twins have other, more permanent distinguishing features, but once they take the ice at Young Arena, few people are likely to confuse them. For nearly as long as they have played the game, Matt has been a forward, and Kyle has played defense.

"Matt has always been fast, but he's always working to get that extra step every single season," says Kyle, adding, "Every summer that we've been training together, he's always the one that's pushing me. He's obviously got speed to his game, and he tries to make the players around him better with his vision and playmaking."

For Matt's part, he has had the closest firsthand view of the improvements to Kyle's skills.

"It started with him working on his skating a lot. He makes good first passes out of the zone. He can step up on the rush when he needs to, and he's turning into a shutdown defender as well," says Matt, explaining further, "He takes away passing lanes and isn't afraid to get in front of the puck and block it."

Family has always been important in the Koopmans' hockey careers, and that extends beyond the two brothers themselves. Their father, Doug, was their coach for many of the years they spent learning the game. They also learned from older brothers, Ben (who was recruited to play football at Holy Cross) and Tom.

"Both our older brothers played at Marblehead High School," Kyle noted about the public school in Massachusetts where he and Matt also spent their freshman and sophomore years. "When we were sophomores there, Tom was a senior captain, so that was pretty cool to have the three of us on a team.

"We'd been watching them play, especially our oldest brother [Ben], we'd go to all his games."

"I think we kind of knew going into freshman year that we were probably going to boarding school," Matt adds, "so we definitely wanted to spend a year or two at public school after – like Kyle said – going to games when we were in seventh and eighth grade and watching as part of the big crowds...that's kind of a dream, to be on the varsity team, playing in front of those crowds."

With only a few exceptions during summer sessions, the Koopman twins always played on the same team, and that extended into high school, first at Marblehead and then as upperclassmen at the Berkshire School in Sheffield, Massachusetts. There, they not only played hockey but also spent time on the soccer and baseball teams.

However, last spring, it was not clear that Matt and Kyle would still be teammates. Matt had been on the Black Hawks' affiliate list for a couple of seasons, while Kyle wondered what junior team – and even what league – he might end up with.

"I didn't really know what my future was going to be," remembers Kyle. "I was just really happy when I saw I got drafted by Waterloo…happy obviously with the opportunity that I could keep playing with Matt and not have to split up for the first time."

And if it hadn't turned out that way?

"It's kind of hard to envision," Matt says, as they speculate on whether the two might have even dropped the gloves had they found themselves on opposite sides of a USHL rivalry. "I haven't really thought about it, but I'm sure there'd be some roughness to it."

Instead, they are the latest brother combination to play for the Black Hawks in the same season, joining the likes of Chris and Peter Ferraro, as well as J.P. and Mike Testwuide. The last brother duo simultaneously on the Waterloo roster was James and Mike Marcou in 2006/07.

"Obviously the coaches here have great hockey minds," says Matt. "When they say something, you have to try and be a sponge. I'm trying to be a better defensive player, and offensively as well, they teach us a lot."

At his position, Kyle has also been absorbing a lot of lessons since arriving in September.

"Learning little details that make defensemen get to that next level…little things like keeping good gaps and what to do with your stick, different skating techniques…since getting here, I've been working hard to try and make myself better in those areas. It's starting to pay off, but there's still a lot of work to be done with my skating and getting pucks through at the point."

On the blue line, Kyle has played in every game and has four assists. Up front, Matt has appeared in 17 of 19 matchups so far. He scored his first goal against the Fargo Force on November 4th.

One thing for which the Koopmans had a short adjustment period was living away from home. They credit their time at boarding school.

"In public school you've been growing up with the same kids your whole life," says Kyle. "At boarding school, every year they're bringing in new people in all grades."

"We had 20-something or 30 countries represented at our school," interjects Matt. "Moving away from home at our age, I think it was good for us to go there and develop as a hockey player and as a student and a person."

Waterloo is quite a bit farther from home than the three-hour drive from Marblehead to the Berkshire School. For the two boys with tight family ties, the Black Hawks' housing program has provided a surrogate family, now that their parents aren't able to drive to games each weekend.

The twins' mom and dad have had the chance to watch them play in Waterloo already, and later this season, older brothers Ben and Tom hope to make it to the Cedar Valley as well to watch the little brothers who were once in the stands cheering for them.

"They did their best to make it out to some of our games at Berkshire," Kyle says, "and it was always a good time after a game when you'd look up, and you'd see your oldest brother who drove three hours out to come watch you play in the middle of the wintertime."

And in the years to come, it will be easier for the Koopman family to gather at the rink. From Waterloo, Matt and Kyle will continue skating together in the NCAA at Providence College, just an interstate highway trip down the road from Marblehead.

A Klee Family Thanksgiving

Three Klee brothers played in the USHL, with two of them spending time in Waterloo. Garrett Klee talked about his experience while at Young Arena to watch David. The story appeared on waterlooblackhawks.com on November 23, 2022.

On Thursday, hundreds of Cedar Valley families will take out the nice dishes and cloth napkins, roast a turkey and mash some potatoes, watch a nap-worthy football game, then come to Young Arena for the day's main event.

This week's Thanksgiving game will be the 51st played in Waterloo and the 22nd between the Black Hawks and the Cedar Rapids RoughRiders. Forward Garrett Klee was involved in two of those earlier games. In 2016, the Hawks scratched out a 1-0 win, then in 2017, Klee and his teammates enjoyed a more comfortable 5-2 result. Like so many others at the rink on Thursday, Klee will be on hand with his family, even though he wouldn't have anticipated that just a month ago.

Starting in 2015 as a member of the Madison Capitols, the Colorado native played in 160 USHL regular season games. He was with the Hawks for his final two junior seasons and served as Waterloo's captain in 2017/18, when the team earned the Anderson Cup with the league's best regular season record. Klee committed to Northern Michigan, spending four years in the Wildcats program and becoming a fixture in the lineup.

After finishing his eligibility in Marquette, pro hockey was the ideal next step to stay in the game. Northern Michigan's season ended just in time for Klee to take the ice a few times at the ECHL level last spring.

"I got to go play a couple games for Kansas City on the road in Rapid City and then went back to school, because I had to finish up some classes and graduate," Klee says, adding that his hope had been to establish a fulltime presence with the Mavericks in 2022/23.

"I was there [at training camp] for two months, and a numbers game happened. Unfortunately, I was released, so now we're just keeping our options open and hopefully figuring out a new home."

In the meantime, Klee has spent recent days in Waterloo training and watching his younger brother, Black Hawks rookie David Klee. This isn't the first time he has been back at Young Arena for a family connection. Middle brother Mason was a member of the Sioux Falls Stampede when the South Dakota-based club matched up with the Hawks in the 2019 playoffs. If there were any divided loyalties in that situation, there are none now. Garrett can cheer for both his younger brother and his former team without conflict.

David had actually played during last season's Thanksgiving game as part of a six-game stint off the Hawks' affiliate list. This year, he has appeared in 13 of Waterloo's 15 games, producing his first USHL goal last weekend. David was also noted as a prospect for the 2023 NHL Draft by NHL Central Scouting earlier this fall.

"He's a big forward and can use his body to protect the puck like I did, and he's got a little bit more finishing touch and finesse," says Garrett. "He's smart with the puck and patient, like my middle brother. That little finish flair…that's pretty much just him. I don't think anyone else in the Klee family has that."

Garrett also provided some background on David's nickname: Bugs.

"He started off as a 'Bugaboo' when he was a baby, and then it just transformed into 'Bugs' and that's how he's known all around our family and our friends and everyone."

Other members of the Klee family have also gravitated into town in time for the holiday. Although there is no shortage of familiar faces when Garrett comes to the rink, some of them are only two dimensional.

"You expect to see your teammates [in person], but you see [Jackson] Cates' picture up on the wall. [Jack] Drury, all those guys that have gone on, and you're just happy for them. Triggs [Bobby Trivigno] obviously had a great career in college, so did Waiter [Garrett Wait], and I still talk with them.

"With all the social media, snap chats, and all that, we have a big group chat where we still talk, flip crap at each other, and just stay connected. That's the key."

Klee says those connections were relatively easy to maintain while everyone was playing college hockey, regardless of whether the former Hawks were attending the same school.

"I got to play again with [Mason] Palmer and Hank [Sorensen] and then play against a bunch of other teammates like Backy [Solag Bakich] and all those guys. You just laugh about the old times, and make sure everyone's still healthy and happy and doing their thing.

"The biggest thing you take away from anywhere is your teammates and those relationships that you build with the guys," Klee explains. "That's really the thing you miss most as a player: that camaraderie of coming to the rink every day, working hard and battling with each other, and then at the end of the day, you're all still best buddies."

Klee says he is looking forward to being back in that environment – wherever that might be – as he waits for his next opportunity in pro hockey.

"There's not a lot of spots available. [On the ice] as a player, you just have to stay patient…you're in the lineup, you're not. This is the same thing. You just stay patient and bide your time. Wait for an opportunity, and then hopefully an opportunity presents itself, and you can capitalize on it. And that's pretty much what I'm doing now. Just trying to stay patient, staying in shape, and being ready if I get an opportunity."

In the meantime, being in Waterloo with family for Thanksgiving is a pretty good option.

"It was really fun to play on Thanksgiving as a player. That was the game you had circled on your calendar. Now getting to watch it, you know it's a little more nerve-wracking when you have no control over what happens in the game, but it's going to be fun."

Generations of Waterloo hockey fans who have been coming back for Thanksgiving year after year couldn't agree more.

Home For Christmas (But Not Much More)

The Iowa Sports Connection *printed this reflection on the USHL's fleeting Christmas breaks in Volume 9, Issue 11 – February, 2008.*

The bus ride from Indianapolis to Waterloo takes seven hours...unless snow is falling and the lines on Interstate 74 dissolve into the slush. In that case, add three hours more. It seems longer when the bus is weaving, trying to find traction on invisible pavement, and when the end of the trip means the beginning of Christmas break.

The Waterloo Black Hawks pulled into the Young Arena parking lot just before 8 a.m. on December 16th, after a 5-4 comeback win against the Indiana Ice the night before. Driving back through the snow storm after a loss would have been really miserable.

Most of the players weren't done traveling when the bus ride ended. The United States Hockey League offers the top level of competition for pre-college players, who come from all over the country to prove themselves. Some were on the highway again as soon as their cars had warmed. Others dashed to make flights out of Waterloo and Cedar Rapids that would have been easy to catch with three extra hours.

Forward Brett Olson went home from Waterloo to Superior, Wisconsin, just across the St. Louis River from Duluth. Goalie Matt DiGirolamo jetted to Penllyn, Pennsylvania. Defenseman Chad Billins skipped the trip back to Waterloo altogether and drove from Indianapolis to Marysville, Michigan.

"We ended up staying the night in [Indianapolis] because the roads were pretty bad," Billins said. His family had traveled from northeast of Detroit to watch the games in Indiana. "It was a little slow getting home; it took a couple hours more than normal, but once we got into Michigan the roads were pretty clear."

Billins admitted he was excited to go home for Christmas. During the 2006/07 season he had played junior hockey in Alpena, Michigan, on the northwest edge of Lake Huron. Further from Marysville this year, the holiday break offered a rare opportunity to see family and friends.

Brett Olson is in his third season with the Black Hawks and serves as team captain. He knew how to make to most of his limited time in Superior over the holidays.

"For me, I just try to spend time with my family during the day, and then at night after my friends get off work – and some of them still have school up until that Thursday and Friday [the 20th and 21st] with finals and stuff – then you go hang out with them when you have time."

That's with room built into the schedule for skating and workouts. Although there were no USHL games from December 16th through the 27th, the league was approaching the midpoint of its season. Coaches stressed the importance of remaining in game condition and encouraged players to work with their old high school or midget teams while away on "break." With the first league games after the holiday scheduled for Friday, December 28th, the first post-Christmas practice in Waterloo was at 6 p.m. on the 26th.

"I think everybody was kind of ready to go," Olson said. "They were ready to come back and start playing again. You're away from it a little bit and you miss it."

Even so, few if any of the Black Hawks were willing to travel back to Iowa on Christmas itself, setting up a hectic race back for practice on Boxing Day.

"Coming back here was a nightmare," recalled Matt DiGirolamo, who flew back from eastern Pennsylvania. "It was snowing in Minneapolis and I guess it was snowing here as well. Our plane from Philadelphia to Minneapolis got delayed three hours, and when I finally got to Minneapolis, we got delayed another two hours to Waterloo."

DiGirolamo said he was a little nervous about the connecting flight to Waterloo through bad weather in a small commuter plane, but the trip was safe, and he was even at practice on time.

"I actually felt like we picked up right where we left off," DiGirolamo said.

The results when play resumed seemed to prove DiGirolamo right. The Black Hawks beat the Lincoln Stars 3-2 on December 28th. Olson scored the first goal of the night and set up the game-winner. Billins was also on the ice for two of Waterloo's three goals. DiGirolamo enjoyed an evening off after playing in five of the Hawks' previous six games.

The new year is when the USHL schedule gets tougher. From the beginning of January until mid-April, the Black Hawks won't have more than five days between games. They'll play every Friday and Saturday. And don't forget about practice.

Hectic cross-country travel might sound easy by season's end.

Crease to Coach

Motte Returns for Black Hawks Camps

Many players find their way back onto Young Arena ice in the years after they have moved on from Waterloo. C.J. Motte is among them, as he shared in the Preseason 2018 issue of Hawk Tawk Mag-e-Zine.

Not all of C.J. Motte's accomplishments in Waterloo came with a goalie glove, or with a hockey stick in his hands.

"Halfway through my second year [2010/11], we helped tear out the old lockers and had a little bit of fun with a sledgehammer knocking those down. It was a team-building thing as well, bringing all the new stalls off the truck that got delivered."

The major renovations at Young Arena that fall changed the look of the Black Hawks' locker room, while also adding the team's "Hockey Central" meeting area/classroom and providing additional office space. The project also presaged a host of developments and improvements in downtown Waterloo in the blocks surrounding the rink.

Coming back as a Black Hawks alumnus, Motte has noticed the changing landscape.

"You've got the new Sportsplex which has been added since I was here. You've got the college and apartments. They're just sprucing up and making everything look nicer."

Yet Motte can still find his way back to the arena. Perhaps that is because he has returned to Waterloo more often than nearly any of his contemporaries who played here near the beginning of the decade. Over the last two years, his trips to the Cedar Valley have covered relatively short distances while he played pro hockey in nearby cities.

Before disbanding as a member club within the ECHL, the Quad Cities Mallards provided Motte a home, although he was called up to patrol the crease for several American Hockey League teams, including the Iowa Wild. During the coming year, he will have the chance to win a regular roster spot with Iowa. If he does, it may mean a less nomadic lifestyle; during Motte's pro career, he has spent time with seven teams in just over three seasons.

"It really goes down to your contract," he explains, "If you're signed with a specific American League team or NHL team, you only get called up throughout their system. Even though Quad Cities was affiliated with the Chicago Wolves and Vegas last year, I was only signed with Quad Cities, so that gave me the range to go to any American team that needed a goalie.

"That gave me the opportunity to spend a few months with the Chicago Wolves and a couple months with the Iowa Wild and a few weeks in Stockton [with the Heat], and really [they were] different experiences in every place, but I enjoyed all of them."

Along with close proximity during at least part of the winter, Motte has returned to Waterloo in the summertime to help with a variety of Black Hawks camps. Starting in late July, the Hawks' coaching staff relied on him to work with dozens of young players at all positions during "Futures" gatherings for 13- through 15-year-olds. Motte stuck around into the new month as candidates for the 2018/19 Black Hawks roster arrived in town.

"I don't feel like I'm that much older than the guys out there on the ice. I've been helping coach camp, and even when I'm out there I still feel like 'Hey, I want to get out there and participate in camp,' so I think still playing helps me relate," Motte says, adding, "Hopefully my experiences can help translate to their game now…help them, encourage them, give them a few words of wisdom that they can go forward with."

The 27-year-old also gets a boost from his visits to Waterloo that he hopes will carry into the coming season.

"Being back here at camp, just the energy level, the passion…everyone's just trying to make the team, plus play on after. I just really feel some excitement for myself," Motte says. "These guys are out here trying to make the team and [make] the most of their opportunity, which is exactly what I'm trying to do with the Wild.

"They'll also teach you quite a bit. They'll ask you questions or they'll point out things: 'Hey I did this. Should I have done this?' And you can have a little dialog with them and, you know, they'll see the game differently than you do, especially me being a goaltender. I always watch it from my specific spot [in the crease], so seeing it while coaching from the bench, you see a few different things. Plus talking to the forwards and defensemen on the bench all the time about different plays and systems…you get to see how they see the game and how it's different from your [perspective]."

Ultimately, the environment Motte will step into next month in Des Moines will be much like this month's Black Hawks camp in Waterloo.

"It's absolutely similar. There's passion, there's grit in both. Obviously here in the USHL, the kids are a little younger than the professional ranks, so there's mistakes made, but hockey's a game of mistakes, so they're made everywhere."

Regardless of the age or skill level of the players, or even the time of year, Motte says some things are universal in the sport.

"Overall, you talk to a hockey guy anywhere, whether you run into him in Waterloo, Des Moines, or somewhere in Europe, you're going to have a lot to talk about. Hockey guys tend to stick together and are usually really good people."

From Goalie to Foodie

Former goalie Parker Milner offered the details about his unique career in a March 4, 2022 waterlooblackhawks.com feature.

Even before he came to Waterloo in 2008, Parker Milner's interest in food stretched well beyond red sauce, alfredo, and the tasty but recurring-ad-nauseum breadsticks from Fazoli's, which seemed to be part of every Black Hawks road trip at that time.

Milner says that as a youth hockey player, he was already encouraging his friends to be more adventurous with their pregame meals.

"I remember on hockey trips, just trying to get not only my teammates but their parents to try some of the places [my family] was eating. It was often a challenge," he admits.

While growing up in Pittsburgh, Milner's own taste horizons were pushed far afield from Primanti Bros. sandwiches. He credits family trips to far away destinations in Europe and South America, and the influence of his father, for giving him a different perspective on food than the typical adolescent.

"When we were going on hockey trips, my dad would find these different restaurants for us to go to. He always wanted me to try different kinds of food," says Milner. "He had been working in New York City for a number of years and had grown more interested in their restaurant scene and been involved there.

"That really stayed with me."

Milner was 18 during his one and only season with the Black Hawks. Waterloo won 37 games in 2008/09, with Milner in net for 20 of those victories, including three shutouts. During the four years that followed, he was a member of two NCAA National Championship teams at Boston College, including 2012 when he was named Most Outstanding Player of the Frozen Four.

During the rest of the 2010s, Milner played professionally in the AHL and ECHL, taking the ice for over 300 regular season and playoff games with seven different clubs. He was on rosters for teams as distant as Stockton, California, and Bridgeport, Connecticut. Milner's longest stay was with the ECHL's Charleston-based South Carolina Stingrays.

Today he remains a professional in Charleston, although he has set aside his mask and goalie pads for a new vocation. Last October, he was named Food Editor for the local daily paper, *The Post and Courier*.

"It is a pretty charmed life; I feel incredibly fortunate," says Milner about trading one dream career for another.

Although Milner was having a solid season in 2019/20, he was also contemplating life after sports. His 2.20 goals-against average ranked second in the league, and Milner had a 20-6-3 record when the season ended early due to the coronavirus.

"The more I went along in the professional hockey ranks, the more important it was to me to have something off the ice that I really cared about as well. I felt that it freed me up on the ice and just made me feel present."

At Boston College, Milner had studied business rather than journalism, adding an extra layer of learning between the crease and the newspaper copy desk. First casually, then in more formal settings, he had begun writing about restaurants and enjoyable meals while he was still playing.

"When I got to Charleston, I applied for a job with Eater, which is a national online brand. I sent in some samples I had written for a freelance position, and I was lucky enough to have them get back to me. I just, sort of built it up organically from there."

Milner says he also interned for *Charleston Magazine* and took writing classes in the years prior to his hockey retirement.

Ahead of the pandemic in early 2020, he had made a definitive step toward a future of mixing food and words, accepting a second job with the weekly *Charleston City Paper*.

"I had started that job parttime for about three weeks during the season, and then all of the sudden the season was over, and I was just right into it," Milner says.

There was a lot to cover. As public health officials across the country grappled with COVID-19, restaurants were pushed to serve their customers in dramatically different ways. Considerable creativity was required to keep the doors open, especially as dine-in service came to a complete halt. In a dynamic, oceanside metro like Charleston, restaurants are a significant attraction.

Milner says residents and visitors there enjoy a range of culinary options.

"Southern cuisine definitely has its 'heavy hitter' dishes that people always look for: shrimp and grits, she-crab soup, fried chicken, okra soup. Those sorts of things are very popular here. But being in a big city like Charleston with lots of people who come from other big cities and other places and other countries, there's really a nice mix of food and restaurants to try."

As Milner sees it, his role is to try that food, share the experience, and tell the stories of the people who make it. It's not about rating what's good or bad.

"That's the assumption: that every food writer is a food critic, and I'm not," says Milner, elaborating, "I'm doing feature stories, I'm going to restaurants and talking about the food, of course, but it's more explaining what the food tastes like, where it comes from, why the chef did this, what is influencing the dishes that he's serving, as opposed to strict reviews."

He admits there are things in recipes he is not excited to see. Topping that list: sour cream.

"It's a good reminder to me that even someone who likes to pride themselves on trying everything…sometimes you get a mental block. If you push through that, it's just like in hockey: if you have a mental block about a skill or something that you can't quite master, you just attack it head on. You start to forget that the sour cream is there, you start to forget that the skill that you've struggled with for so long is something that you've struggled with."

As for the indelible food impressions from his time as a Black Hawk, Milner was sorry to learn that the Boardwalk Deli on East 4th Street closed some years ago. He and teammates ate scores of sandwiches there each week, with one cold cut combination – the Lee Moffie Special – continuing to bear the name of Milner's teammate long after Moffie had moved on to the University of Michigan.

However, if Milner returned to Waterloo today, he knows he could find a sandwich that is even better.

"DeeDee VanBesien's food was incredible every night," he says of the billet mom he lived with. "I remember these roast beef sandwiches right at the front of my mind, and also this bread she made, called 'friendship bread,' that was absolutely delicious. It was something that Eddie Olczyk [Jr.] and I would horde on the road trips."

Black Hawks on the Job

Hockey Players at Work, Then and Now

Hawks fans had access to this feature from waterlooblackhawks.com beginning in August, 2025.

Away from the rink and out of context, even the veteran captain of the Waterloo Black Hawks can still enjoy a degree of anonymity in the Cedar Valley.

Reid Morich and teammate Brock Schultz blended right in as they worked parttime hours last season at a large retailer in Cedar Falls. Some of the responsibilities were behind-the-scenes. A truck full of merchandise would arrive, then Morich, Schultz, and other employees would unload it and organize the contents to be moved up front. Extra stock would be arranged in back so it could be rolled to the sales floor later. And at times during the approximately three days per week when they were on the clock, Morich and Schultz would inevitably encounter customers with questions about where to find an item or whether the store carried a particular product.

"I never did have a fan recognize me," says Morich. "One thing that Brock and I got laugh out of when we saw customers wearing Black Hawks merchandise was walking up to them and asking if they needed help finding anything in the store. This happened a few times, but not one person recognized us.

"I guess it's hard to recognize us without having a number and a helmet on."

Not many other Black Hawks spent their "free time" away from Young Arena involved in gainful employment. The two 19-year-olds were not taking online high school classes. They also found a manager willing to work with their tricky – sometimes unpredictable – schedules.

"I wanted to keep myself productive," Morich explains. "I liked that it gave me structure to my days. It also made me appreciate the afternoons that I had off, because I could stay longer at the rink with my teammates or relax at home."

Being "on the clock" may be noteworthy for a Waterloo hockey player in 2025, but it is nothing new. As the *Waterloo Courier* explained while introducing local readers to the United States Hockey League in October 1962, "In the U.S. circuit the teams only play twice a week and all the members of the squads have other fulltime jobs…The majority of the players who come here for the training camp come with the understanding that if they make the team a job will be found for them."

Waterloo's earliest hockey players provided a boost to the local workforce. Multiple members of that team worked at Powers Manufacturing or Hawkeye Steel or John Deere. Some who chose to remain in the community put college degrees to use and established long careers. For example, goalie Jim Coyle joined Iowa Public Service and rose to an executive position as that utility company evolved to become MidAmerican Energy. Defenseman Bernie Nielsen found a job as an industrial engineer for a company which made valves and industrial controls in Marshalltown. Into the early 1970s, Nielsen made a 100-mile loop from Marshalltown to Waterloo and back for games and practices.

Dave Swick had been involved in a monumental project while he was approximately the same age as today's Black Hawks players. As a young iron worker in the 1950s, Swick was part of the 3,500-man crew building the Mackinac Bridge, which carries Interstate 75 for nearly five miles while connecting Michigan's upper and lower peninsulas. Coming to Waterloo in 1963, the forward found work with Jens Olesen Construction, working at project sites like Crossroads Mall and other major building efforts. He became a supervisor, applying some of the lessons he learned to later stints as head coach for the Black Hawks and the Waterloo Warriors high school team.

"Iron workers are rough. They work hard, but they play hard too. So you know, you got to keep on your toes, because they were good bunch of guys, but you got to watch them," says Swick. "Hockey players may be a little like that…You really can't show [iron workers or hockey players] the true side of you. They have to think that you're a little ornery sometimes."

The Hawks' original player/coach was an entrepreneur. Oakie Brumm operated a concrete construction business in Marquette, Michigan. The seasonal nature of construction – especially so far north – allowed Brumm to manage his work crews in the summer and the Black Hawks in the winter with limited conflicts. Bud McRae took over from Brumm as player/coach at the rink and also worked in a management role for Continental Western Life Insurance's Waterloo office. He later went into business for himself as proprietor of the Hat Trick Lounge. Jim Smith (Smitty's) and Paul Johnson (Paulie's Place) also opened popular watering holes, often connecting with local hockey fans in new ways.

Brian "Duke" Dutkowski connected with some of the Black Hawks' younger fans. The education major at Colorado College didn't arrive early enough in the winter of 1962/63 to put his teacher training to use in a classroom of his own, but he was leading a world history class at Columbus Catholic High School by the following fall, as well as working as an assistant football coach. A few years later, John Lesyshen would represent the Hawks in Waterloo's public school system. The University of North Dakota graduate went on to a long career as a principal and administrator. During the 1970s, defenseman Charlie Brown and forward Cam McGregor took short term positions moving from class to class as substitute teachers.

Goalie George McPhee was also a Waterloo educator in the 1970s, a novel use of his accounting degree from Boston College. McPhee decided that work as an accountant wasn't for him, so he taught the subject at Hawkeye Institute of Technology, today's Hawkeye Community College.

"I was very familiar with performing on the ice but was unprepared for having to be prepared to 'perform' as a teacher," says McPhee. "My learning curve was pretty difficult that first year. I wish I had done a better job for my students. However, with each subsequent year of experience I became a more competent teacher. Those long hockey bus rides became teaching prep time for the classroom.

"Over these last 50 years as a Black Hawk alum, I have really benefited from the teaching experience I acquired while living in Waterloo…I eventually became a residential painting contractor. I found my teaching experience valuable in training new employees."

Defenseman Paul Wormith was one of McPhee's teammates and also came from a prestigious eastern school. Perhaps Wormith's philosophy degree from Brown helped him to better appreciate his sometimes-cushy work as assistant maintenance man at the Ramada Inn.

"I mostly fixed things and painted rooms," Wormith says. "The job was great, because I had a master key for all the rooms, so if I needed a nap, I had lots of quiet places to rest during the day, and the unlimited, free lunch buffet was even better for a young 22-year-old with a big appetite for food.

"The general manager of the hotel and the maintenance supervisor were very good to me, because they were big fans of the hockey team, and they seemed to really like me. Despite my naps and big appetite, they knew they could trust me to always get my assignments done each day. It also turned out to be good training for my later career as a restoration contractor back in Canada."

Forward Stan Blom knew precisely what he wanted to do after hockey. Playing for the Black Hawks – then working for the team as an assistant coach – helped him bide his time until he came to the top of the hiring list for the St. Paul Fire Department.

"You've got to learn to live with people, and everyone has got a different personality, and that's just how it is in hockey," explains Blom. "My whole life in hockey has taught me those benefits, getting along, and everyone is a little different, and just accepting it. It's helped me out through life."

Blom's time with the Black Hawks corresponded with the transition to junior hockey in the late 1970s. Coach Jack Barzee helped to scout out jobs for the young players coming to town, including Ron Milardo, who worked for Palace Clothiers.

"There were 12 of us that lived at 408 Vermont Street, and we had a blast in 78/79. I had one of the few cars, so I was always the one taking everyone to work," explains Milardo. "Working was a way of life for all of us to support ourselves, and we shared cooking duties and cleaning the house. I will say that we had a booster club that supported us with dinners and food occasionally. We also had the Hat Trick Lounge that was a frequent spot to have a beer" *[Note: the legal drinking age at that time was still 18]*.

Bill Grillo followed Milardo to both the Black Hawks and Palace Clothiers, but didn't have his own car during the 1979/80 season.

"I would have to take the bus to work and back. There was this really nice female co-worker who had a boyfriend. The two of them would often give me a ride home at night after we closed. Problem was, he had a Chevy Corvette and fitting three people in that vehicle was next to impossible," Grillo remembers, adding, "Every time you are thrust into a situation with complete strangers, such as a new bunch of teammates or a new group of work associates, it makes us a little uncomfortable, but that's when we learn and grow."

The 1980s and early 90s came with economic challenges in the Cedar Valley which made it difficult for Black Hawks players to find even parttime jobs. Coupled with an increased focus on college prep, work away from the rink became rarer, but never disappeared completely. Andy Roach spent two seasons with the Hawks in the early 1990s.

"I remember working with Ben MacLennan at an office furniture store called Kirk Gross every morning from about 8 to 12 before practice," says Roach. "Ben had to deliver some office furniture one morning with the big delivery truck. I asked him to stop at the drive-through at Burger King on his way back and pick me up some breakfast.

"Now Ben was not the type of guy who would do something personal while he is supposed to be working. Well, to make a long story short, Ben came back to the warehouse with my breakfast, but also explained to me that he drove the work truck into the overhang at the Burger King drive-thru."

If Roach's teammate Todd Steinmetz ever drove the big box trucks for the Northeast Iowa Food Bank, Steinmetz kept their vehicles out of the drive-thru. He spent most of his time putting together pallets of food and supplies which were delivered to food pantries throughout the region.

"I would go straight to practice at 1 p.m. after work. Our coach, Scott Mikesch, encouraged us to work or go to school when we played," remembers Steinmetz. "I really enjoyed working at the Food Bank. The people were great to work with. I used to give tickets to an older fellow named Vern that also worked there."

Into more recent decades, the willingness to work has continued, although sometimes with snags. One Canadian player accepted an offer to move behind the counter at a favorite sandwich shop. He liked the job and it went well for several days until the store manager needed to process payroll. The player did not have a social security number, nor did he have a visa allowing him to accept paid employment. That player and the restaurant mutually agreed to part ways and avoid any entanglements with federal labor rules.

On the other hand, forward Paul Weisgarber successfully navigated two different jobs during his two seasons with the Black Hawks. After a year washing cars for minimum wage as a local dealership's 'Automotive Exterior Maintenance Specialist,' Weisgarber enjoyed a relative windfall the next year as part of a construction crew.

"That job paid something like $9 per hour, which at the time felt like I'd hit the lottery. I typically worked from 7:30 to 11:30 a.m. for both jobs, which fit well before our practice schedule," notes Weisgarber, who can also share a cautionary story which is funny in hindsight, "I was still wearing our team-issued gym shoes to work (not exactly OSHA compliant), and one day I stepped on a rusted nail that went straight through the sole and into my foot. TK [Trainer Todd Klein] wasn't thrilled, especially since it meant a tetanus shot right before a game. The silver lining? I showed up Monday morning to find a proper pair of work boots waiting for me, courtesy of the site manager.

"Those jobs taught me how to manage time and energy: juggling early mornings, physical work, and the demands of high-level hockey," added Weisgarber. "Just as important, they gave me a sense of what real work feels like. That perspective stayed with me, especially as I moved into academic and professional roles where effort still determines progress."

Morich echoes those feelings about getting a so-called real job.

"It forces you to have structure and discipline outside of the rink," he says. "Maybe wait until October or November so you can enjoy the warm weather, but once it's cold and there's not much to do, it gets you out of your room and off of the video games…I met a ton of great people that I'll never forget, and they made my junior hockey experience that much more enjoyable."

And he met a few Black Hawks fans with no idea who was helping them cross off the items on their shopping list.

www.ingramcontent.com/pod-product-compliance
Lightning Source LLC
LaVergne TN
LVHW010618100826
845148LV00014B/3025

* 9 7 9 8 2 1 8 7 6 9 3 4 5 *